Melodic Clawhammer Banjo

By Ken Perlman

Front cover banjo: Primrose, model
Back cover banjo: Hummingbird
Courtesy of OME banjos, www.omebanjos.com

Edited by Brenda Murphy
Book design by Geralyne Lewandowski
Interior photos: Chuck Fishbein (technical)
pg.22 Courtesy John Edwards Memorial Foundation,
pg.33 David Gahr, pg.35 Georgia Sheron,pg.40 Diana J. Davies,
pg.57 Wren D'Antonio, pg.74 Eric Valdina
pg. 79 John Cohen, pg.84 Julia Fahey

ISBN 978-1-57424-202-7

Acknowledgements

Thanks for information and anecdotes:
-to Dan Collins, Rich Nevins, and Bill Ochs (Irish tunes)
-to Jim Morrison (English, Scottish, and New England tunes)
-to Hank Sapoznik (Southern tunes)
-to Peter Hoover, Ray Alden, and Hank Sapoznik (Banjo History, playing styles,
 and lore)
Special thanks to Hank Sapoznik for his general help and encouragement.
Thanks to Ron Osborne for some helpful writing hints.
Thanks to the following New York area musicians who dug deep into their record
libraries to find some tune sources for me: Bill Christoperson, Art Friedman,
Scott Kellogg, Kevin Krajick, Matt Oppenheimer, Steve Uhrik, and Fred Winter.

CD Track List

Track 1 - Old Joe Clarke
Track 2 - Shady Grove
Track 3 - Cripple Creek
Track 4 - Double Thumbing Exercise
Track 5 - Boatman
Track 6 - Georgia Railroad
Track 7 - The Ways of the World
Track 8 - Sandy River Belle
Track 9 - Old Mother Flanagan
Track 10 - Dry and Dusty
Track 11 - Frosty Morning
Track 12 - The Eighth of January
Track 13 - The Year of Jubilo
Track 14 - Jimmy in the Swamp
Track 15 - The West Fork Gals
Track 16 - Salt River
Track 17 - Kitchen Girl
Track 18 - The Avalon Quickstep
Track 19 - Colored Aristocracy
Track 20 - The Clinch Mountain Backstep
Track 21 - The Cherokee Shuffle
Track 22 - Ragtime Annie
Track 23 - Blackberry Blossom
Track 24 - Whiskey Before Breakfast
Track 25 - Campbell's Farewell to Redgap
Track 26 - Nancy
Track 27 - A Farewell to Whiskey

Track 28 - Petronella
Track 29 - Balleydesmond Polkas, One
Track 30 - Balleydesmond Polkas, Two
Track 31 - The Linnet
Track 32 - The Lamplighter's Hornpipe
Track 33 - Old French
Track 34 - The Morpath Rant
Track 35 - Clara's Hornpipe
Track 36 - The Rights of Man
Track 37 - President Garfield's Hornpipe
Track 38 - The Tailor's Twist
Track 39 - The Temperance Reel
Track 40 - Farrell O'Gara's Favorite
Track 41 - The Musical Priest
Track 42 - The Mason's Apron
Track 43 - Ships Are Sailing
Track 44 - Rakish Paddy
Track 45 - Behind the Bush in the Garden
Track 46 - The Swallowtail Jig
Track 47 - The Blarney Pilgram
Track 48 - Banish Misfortune
Track 49 - Chamberlin Road
Track 50 - Kemp's Jig
Track 51 - Planxty Lord Inchiquin
Track 52 - O'Carolan's Concerto
Track 53 - The Mineola Rag
Track 54 - Tenor Chorale Theme from
            Cantata # 140 by J.S Bach

Contents

Introduction

Melodic clawhammer is a style that treats banjo as a complete instrument. Although clawhammer players have traditionally limited themselves to providing rhythmic background for fiddlers and players of other instruments, many modern pickers see no reason to confine themselves to this role. By expanding the range and flexibility of traditional clawhammer techniques, these modern players have, in recent years, been able to develop a totally melodic style of clawhammer. It is called "melodic style" because it enables the clawhammerer to play the complete melodies of fiddle tunes and other types of music.

This book is designed to present a comprehensive, step-by-step approach to melodic clawhammer banjo playing. It is not for total beginners, but just about every other clawhammerer should find this book useful. Intermediate or even near-beginner frailers will be able to use it to teach themselves the skills that go into fine melodic picking. Advanced clawhammerers will find the varied selection of tunes presented here both interesting and challenging.

For the intermediate player, I've broken down melodic clawhammering into a series of basic techniques. These techniques are introduced one at a time with each receiving a detailed explanation and as many illustrations as are necessary to get the point across. A tune making use of each new skill then follows the explanation. Just a few of the areas covered are: hammer-ons, pull-offs, slides, double thumbing, alternate string hammer-ons and pull-offs, triplets, syncopation, rolls, fifth string fretting, and ornaments.

For the advanced player, I've included a repertoire that ranges from simple Appalachian fiddle tunes to Irish jigs and reels, from New England hornpipes to some of the most unusual pieces ever arranged for clawhammer. This repertoire also presents quite a variety of meters, tunings, keys, and modes. Each piece was chosen for its tunefulness and for its adaptability to banjo. As a special effort was made to avoid fudging (altering a melody to make it easier for banjo), each arrangement gives the *full* melody of a tune.

For clawhammerers of all levels, I've tried to come up with a clear, easily understandable system of tablature. The greatest fault of early clawhammer books was unclear notation. I managed to teach myself to play from one of these, but the author's confusing tab system often prevented me from learning his arrangements, even when I was familiar with the melody of a tune. As soon as I realized why my progress was so slow, I vowed to some day devise a better system. The result, explained a little further on, should go a long way toward eliminating those "tablature blues."

I started clawhammering during my days in Ithaca, NY. At first, I taught myself from books, but soon realized that I could learn more by watching some of the fine frailers who lived in the area, such as Howie Bursen and Eric Mintz. Nearly everyone played a melodic style up there, so until I moved to New York City in 1973 I was not aware that some pickers considered the melodic approach a form of musical heresy. In fact, the only other melodic player in the New York area at that time was Hank Sapoznik of the Delaware Water Gap String Band. Although Hank and I traded tabs and mutual support, I felt out of place among New York's traditionally oriented musicians. I began to spend a lot of time with Irish musicians,

who were more open to the idea of melodic playing on five-string. I soon grew to love the complex modal tunes of Ireland and spent considerable effort adapting them to clawhammer style. Hank and I talked a lot in those days about getting a melodic clawhammer book together, and even submitted the idea to a few publishers, but nothing came of it. Now, with melodic style accepted in New York and throughout most of the country, the time is ripe for a book of this sort.

I've asked some other melodic players to contribute arrangements to this book so that you can sample clawhammering styles other than my own. These players include Howie Bursen (of Ithaca, NY), Bob Carlin (of Princeton, NJ), Jeff Davis (of Roslyn, NY), Eric Frandsen (of New York, NY), Eric Mintz (of Jackson Heights, NY), and Hank Sapoznik (of Brooklyn, NY). I've given some biographical information on each clawhammerer as well as some notes on his playing style.

Good picking and good luck.

New York, 1979

The Return of Melodic Clawhammer Banjo

When it first appeared in 1979, *Melodic Clawhammer* broke new ground in several ways. It was the first systematic method devoted to playing fiddle tunes in clawhammer style. It was the first modern clawhammer book that offered a coherent approach for playing Celtic and New England reels, hornpipes and jigs. It was also the first clawhammer book to employ an accurate and reliable system of tablature.

I remember very clearly that at first many banjo pickers and students were concerned that the book's repertoire might be too obscure. "Just how did you ever find those tunes?" was a common refrain. I am happy to report, however, that nearly all the tunes in this book have stood the test of time. In fact, many are now considered standards in their respective genres.

The *Melodic Clawhammer* book was widely distributed throughout the 1980s and 90s throughout North America and western Europe, and had a major role in helping me establish myself as a major player and teacher of the style. And I can't tell you how often someone has come up at a performance or workshop to tell me that the arrangements in Melodic Clawhammer had inspired them to become a serious player. So it was a real thrill when Centerstream informed me that they had decided to re-publish the book.

There are really just a few new features to the Centerstream edition. First, I've revised a couple of historical sketches, most notably the section now entitled "Clawhammer Banjo: A Capsule History." I wish I could have done quite a bit more in this vein but it might have meant redesigning significant sections of the book. Second, there's a new cover. The original edition, through what apparently were a series of utter coincidences, featured on the cover a photo of my banjo playing buddy Mac Benford of Trumansburg, New York (Mac tells me that as a result of this cover, for years quite a number of people thought he was me...). For the new edition, for better or worse, I finally get to grace the cover of my own book and Mac can go back, undisturbed, to being himself.

More important, we've updated the companion recording that comes along with *Melodic Clawhammer*. In the original edition, the book was accompanied by one of those flexible vinyl 33 rpm sound-sheets. This sound sheet, which was sewn into the binding and contained maybe eighteen minutes of music, was pretty much designed to self-destruct after just a few plays on an old-fashioned turntable. The new Centerstream edition, on the other hand, comes with a genuine CD that illustrates every tune in the book. Definitely a better deal, I'd say!

Hope you enjoy the tunes!

Ken Perlman
Leominster, Massachusetts

Clawhammer Style

A Capsule History

The playing style we now call clawhammer probably developed centuries ago in West Africa, for use on a family of stringed instruments that were collectively the banjo's ancestors. In the 1840s and 50s, both the banjo and clawhammer (then known as *stroke-style*) became quite popular throughout North America and Western Europe because of their prominence in traveling minstrel shows. These performances involved songs and comic sketches depicting life on the plantation. Interestingly, an examination of banjo instruction books from this period indicates that the playing of jigs, reels and other complicated dance tunes in stroke-style was common practice.

After 1870, a drive to make the banjo more mainstream and "respectable" led to the replacement of stroke-style in urban areas of the U.S. by a style known as classical banjo, which was based on a three-finger plucking technique derived from classical guitar. To make the banjo more like a guitar, frets were added, the location of the fifth string was regularized at the fifth fret, and changes in design were made to allow for increased tension on the head and neck. Classical style dominated urban banjo playing until c. 1915, when public interest gravitated to Dixieland jazz. By 1920, interest in the 5-string banjo in general had gone into sharp decline and most banjos being made were of the four string tenor or plectrum variety.

Both stroke-style and three-finger style banjo playing had become well established in the mountain regions of the American South by the last decades of the 19th century. By the dawn of the recording era, several variants and hybrids of these two styles had also developed, including two-finger picking and the up-pick-down-strum hybrid that we now refer to as "Seeger style." All these styles were represented to some degree in the hillbilly recordings of the 1920s, but - contrary to the general impression nowadays - recordings from that era featuring "pure" stroke-style (known in the mountains by a variety of descriptive names such as "knocking," "rapping," "flailing," and "clawhammer") were in fact rare.

The 5-string banjo re-emerged from obscurity in the early 1940s due primarily to the efforts of two men - Pete Seeger and Earl Scruggs. Through his activities with the Almanac Singers and later the Weavers, Seeger rekindled interest in both folk-songs and banjo-picking among urban youth; his instruction book *How to Play the 5-String Banjo* (1948), served for a generation as virtually the only published guide to the instrument. Scruggs joined Bill Monroe & His Bluegrass Boys in 1943, and soon electrified the South with his syncopated version of three-finger style. By the 1950s, *Scruggs-picking* had almost eclipsed all other styles of banjo playing throughout that region.

Stroke-style banjo was introduced to the urban "folk revival" by Stu Jamieson, whose mentor was Rufus Crisp, a banjo player from the town of Allen in Floyd County, Kentucky. Jamieson was extremely active in the 40s and 50s in both New York City and California, and taught the style - then often referred to as *frailing* because Seeger used that name in his book - to quite a number of students. By the late 1950s and early 60s, many banjoists whose playing was traceable to Jamieson and Crisp - such as Hank Schwarz, Bill Vanaver, and Billy Faier - were working on a fairly elaborate version of the style, including some note-for-note fiddle-tune arrangements. Some of their efforts were recorded on the seminal LP, *Old-Time Banjo Project*.

Beginning in the 1960s, a second stream of stroke-style playing was drawn into the folk revival. For over a decade, scores of young, urban, college educated folk-music enthusiasts in search of musical inspiration had been flocking to Southern old-time music contests - most notably those at Galax, Virginia and Union Grove, North Carolina. As luck would have it, the Galax region was home to a community of excellent old-time fiddlers and stroke-style banjoists, who were quickly adopted as role models by this new generation. The banjo style of this region - best exemplified by such players as Kyle Creed and Fred Cockerham - has since become known as "Round Peak clawhammer." The Round Peak banjo style features great rhythmic drive, but offers the instrument a very specific, somewhat limited role. The banjo player rarely looks to play a stand-alone melody. Instead he or she focuses on providing a powerful background for the fiddle, hitting in the process as many notes of the tune as can be conveniently obtained in a given tuning.

It was right around this period that the word "clawhammer" became firmly established in the folk-revival as the universal term of choice for stroke-style banjo. The first prominent usage of this term in print appeared in two important instruction books, both published in 1968 - Old-Time Fiddle Tunes for Banjo by John Burke, and Old-Time Mountain Banjo by Art Rosenbaum.

Contemporary Melodic Clawhammer developed in the 1960s and 70s, and has roots firmly in both the Jamieson/Crisp and Round Peak traditions. From the former comes the idea of adapting the techniques of stroke-style to playing note-for-note versions of fiddle tunes; from the latter comes the strong, highly rhythmic attack that brings these versions to life. Two pioneers of the melodic style were the aforementioned Burke and Rosenbaum. By the early 70s, a number of young players were working on pushing out the boundaries of the style; one result was the release in 1976 by Kicking Mule Records of an important LP called (you guessed it!) *Melodic Clawhammer Banjo*, featuring Andy Cahan, Bob Carlin, Dana Loomis, Henry Sapoznik and myself. Some other prominent pickers whose styles of clawhammer have best exemplified melodic playing over the last few decades are Mac Benford, Howie Bursen, Walt Koken, Reed Martin and Michael Miles.

By the 1980s, a watered-down version of Round-Peak clawhammer had evolved in the folk-scene which is sometimes referred to as "festival style." As it spread, an urban legend grew up claiming that festival style was in fact the one and only traditional method of playing old-time banjo.It should be stressed to budding players that festival style is neither more nor less traditional than any of the other approaches to clawhammer that have developed in the folk scene since the 1940s.

Although melodic clawhammer is primarily a solo style, it has sufficient flexibility for use in a variety of contexts. Melodic players can match the fiddler note for note, they can play complex breaks, or they can hang back and play the same supporting role as Round-Peak pickers. They can also function outside a string band context - as backup for vocalists, in various kinds of ensembles, or even (as Michael Miles has shown) as solo instrument fronting a symphony orchestra. In other words, with a little bit of ingenuity, the melodic approach allows the banjo to be adapted to whatever kind of music the musician wants to play on it.

Notation

Tablature

The *tab* will be written on a five-line *staff,* each line corresponding to a banjo string. The first or top line of the staff refers to the first string of the banjo; the fifth or bottom line of the staff indicates the fifth, or *drone* string. A number written on a staff line shows the fret to be pressed down on the corresponding string. So, if the number 3 appears on line two, press down the third fret of the second string. If the number 5 appears on line four, press down the fifth fret of the fourth string.

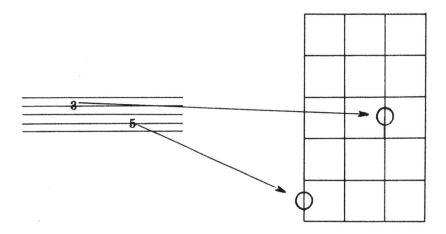

When the number 0 appears on any line, the corresponding string is to be played *open* or unfretted.

The Fifth String

The open fifth string will be notated as 0 even though it begins at the fifth fret. Numbers for *fretted* fifth-string notes, however, will correspond to numbers for fretted long-string notes at the same level on the banjo neck. In other words, fret one of the fifth string will be notated as 6, fret two of the fifth string will be notated as 7, etc.

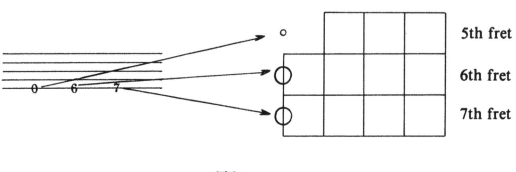

5th fret

6th fret

7th fret

8

Rhythm

By and large, I've borrowed the rhythm notation used in standard music writing, incorporating it into my tab system. Each piece is divided by vertical *barlines* into *measures* (or *bars*) containing equal numbers of *beats.* These groups of beats are organized so that the strongest, the *downbeat,* comes at the beginning of each measure. Any notes occurring just before the first strong beat of a tune are called *pick-up* (or *upbeat* notes) and are clearly set off to the left of the first barline.

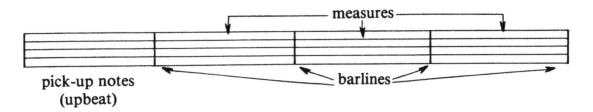

Time

A *time signature* appears at the beginning of every piece to give two kinds of information. The top number tells how many beats occur in each measure of a tune; the bottom number tells what sort of note will be counted as one beat. In the first half of this book, all tunes will bear the time signature $\frac{4}{4}$. This means that every measure contains four beats, and that each quarter note is counted as one beat.

Time values are shown as follows:

0 half note = two beats

2 quarter note = one beat

  quarter rest—don't play for one beat

3 single eighth note = ½ beat (two eighth notes = one quarter note)

  eighth rest—don't play for ½ beat

2 4 beamed eighth notes—often in groups of two or four, connected by a single *beam*

dotted notes—any note with a *dot* after it is lengthened by half again its original value (a dotted half note = 3 beats; a dotted quarter note = 1½ beats; a dotted eighth note = ¾ beat)

 sixteenth note = ¼ beat (four sixteenth notes = one quarter note)

 a "dotted pair" —play these two as eighth notes, with the first receiving much greater duration than the second.

 a triplet—three even notes played in the space of one beat

 grace note—a very quick note, treated as if it had no duration of its own (it "absorbs" some time from the note it is attached to)

double grace note—two very quick notes, considered to have no time value of their own

Methods of Play

Under each note there is a symbol showing how it is to be obtained:

M—downstroke of middle or index fingernail

T— pluck with thumb

H—hammer-on

P—pull-off

SL—slide

qSL—quick slide

When a note is obtained by some action of the fretting hand (H, P, SL, or q SL) it is connected by a tie (⌒) to the note before. If there is a string of H's, P's, or SL's the tie reaches directly from the M-note to the last note of the string.

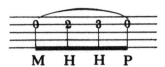

M   H   H   P

Fingering

A Roman numeral above the staff shows the location (or position) of the fretting hand on the fingerboard. In *first position* (I) the fretting hand is located at the *first* fret; then the first finger plays notes on the first fret, the second finger plays notes on the second fret, the third finger plays notes on the third fret, and the fourth finger plays notes on the fourth fret. In *second position* (II) the hand is located at the *second* fret; then the first finger plays notes on the second fret, the second finger plays notes on the third fret, and so on. In *fifth position* (V) the hand is located at the *fifth* fret; then the first finger plays notes on the fifth fret, and so forth. Continue playing in one position until directed to change to another.

Complicated fingering patterns are diagrammed below each piece. A Roman numeral appears at the top of each diagram to indicate position. Note that the diagrams, like the neck of the banjo, bulge out after the fifth fret.

Chords

Sometimes a chord symbol appears above the staff instead of a position numeral. This refers to one of the following chord positions in G tuning.

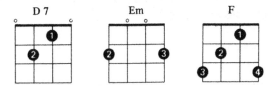

The Barre

Barring involves fretting two or more strings with the flat underside of the first finger. The notation "barre II" indicates that a passage is to be played while the first finger barres across the entire second fret. The notation "½ barre III" shows that a passage is to be played while the first finger barres across two or three strings at the third fret.

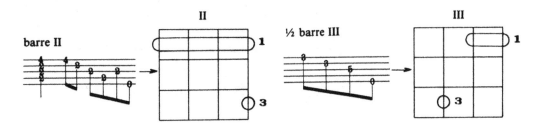

Tunings

I will assume that everyone knows how to get basic G tuning (gDGBD). Other tunings used in this book can be obtained as follows:

Notation	Tuning Name	Directions
gDGCD	sawmill, mountain minor	1) tune to G tuning 2) tune the second string up until its pitch matches that of the fifth fret of the third string
gCGCD	double-C, C-modal	1) tune banjo as for mountain minor 2) tune the fourth string down until the pitch of its seventh fret matches that of the open third string
fCFCD	F tuning	1) tune the banjo as in double-C 2) tune the third string down until its pitch matches that of the fifth fret of the fourth string 3) tune the fifth string down to match the pitch of the third fret of the first string
gCGBD	C tuning	1) tune banjo as for G tuning 2) tune fourth string as for double-C tuning

Repeat Signs

When a tune section is repeated, the symbol ‖: appears at the beginning,* and the symbol :‖ appears at the end.

When the ending of a repeated section is slightly different the second time through, we make use of the following notation:

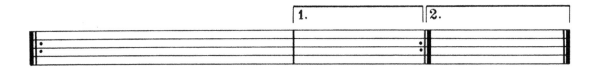

Play through the section until you see the repeat sign, including the measure or measures under bracket number 1 (called the *first ending*); then return to the beginning. The next time through, skip the first ending and play the measure or measures under bracket number 2 (called the *second ending*).

---

*This symbol does not appear at the very beginning of the piece.

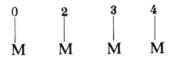

Melodic Clawhammer Technique

The basic motion of clawhammering involves a vertical wrist snap similar to that involved in cracking a whip or casting a fishing line. Each time the wrist snaps down, the middle (or index) fingernail is brought into contact with one of the banjo's four long strings.

wrist snap   recovery

The wrist then brings M back to its original position without producing another note. Since it takes time for the wrist to recover, we can use M only once per beat, making each M-note a quarter note.

```
0     2     3     4
|     |     |     |
|     |     |     |
M     M     M     M
```

The music played in clawhammer style is made up primarily of eighth-note pairs(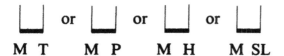).When M plucks a string once per beat, it produces the first note of each pair. To obtain the second note of the pair, other operations must be performed on the strings during the time that M is recovering. These operations include:

plucking the fifth string or one of the three long strings with T
hammering-on
pulling-off
sliding

The notation for runs of eighth-note pairs in clawhammer style, then, is as follows:

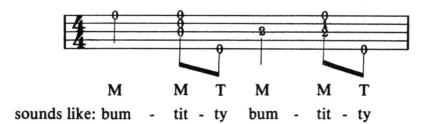

The "Bum-Titty" Strum

This is the basic means of song accompaniment for the frailer. It consists of a quarter note (played by M) followed by two eighth notes (an M-T combination). Ordinarily, this eighth-note pair consists of a *brush* (a downstroke of M that hits several strings) followed by a drone note.

Knockdown Style

Back in the first days of banjo playing, clawhammerers spiced up a popular song by inserting a drone note after each quarter note of the melody. This yielded a series of M-T eighth-note pairs.

Original melody

Melody with added drone notes

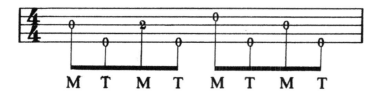

Old Joe Clarke

Below is the fiddle tune "Old Joe Clarke," arranged in *knockdown style*. This is a good opportunity to make sure that all your M-notes and T-notes are exactly even in each eighth-note pair. In other words, each M-note should be allowed to ring exactly one half beat before the T-note is plucked. Each T-note should then be permitted to sound one half beat before the next M-note is plucked, etc. As an aid to playing even M's and T's, try dividing each measure into beats and each beat into half beats. Then count in the following manner: 1 & 2 & 3 & 4 &. Remember that quarter notes get one full beat each (1-&, 2-&) and eighth notes get one half beat (1, &, 2, &).

Hammer-Ons

In a *hammer-on* (H) a finger of the fretting hand strikes, or hammers down on a string plucked by M, making a sound by driving that string against the fingerboard.

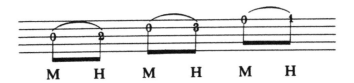

M   H   M   H   M   H

Points to remember about H's:

    —When performing an H, give the string a good thwack with your hammering finger. If you merely place your finger on the string, you won't get sufficient volume.

    —When hammering-on to a fretted string, don't allow the M-note to cease ringing until the H-note begins to sound.

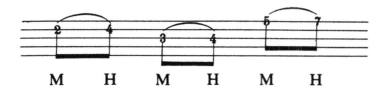

    —Both the M-note and the H-note must be exactly even. Each M-note should ring for one half beat before the hammer-on is performed. Each H-note should sound for one half beat before the next M-note is struck.

Pull-Offs

A *pull-off* (P) is essentially the opposite of a hammer-on. First, M plucks a fretted string. Then, as the finger being used to fret the string is removed from the fingerboard, it catches that string slightly and pulls it in toward the palm in such a way that a clear sound is produced.

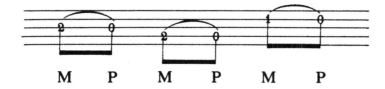

Points to remember about P's:

    —A pull-off is actually more a plucking than a pulling motion. The string should not be drawn in far enough to distort the tone.

    —When pulling-off to a fretted string, make sure that the P-note is securely fretted before the M-note is plucked.

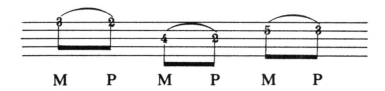

    —When performing a pull-off on strings 2, 3, or 4, special care must be taken to avoid string collisions. In other words, make sure that the pulling finger is drawn in toward the palm at an angle high enough to clear the other strings in its path.

—Both the M-note and the P-note should be exactly even. The M-note should be allowed to ring one half beat before the pull-off is begun. The P-note should sound one half beat before the next M-note is plucked.

Let's put some M-H and M-P combinations to work in an arrangement of "Shady Grove," one of the best-known Appalachian tunes.

Shady Grove

Tuning: g DGCD

Slides

Here M again plucks a fretted string. Then, while the string is still sounding, the fretting finger moves or slides up the fingerboard to a target fret. As the finger performs a *slide* (SL) it must exert enough pressure on the fretboard so that the string never ceases to ring. If a slide is more than one fret in length, move directly to the target fret without hesitating at any of the intervening frets.

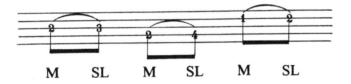

M-notes and SL-notes should be exactly even. Allow the M-note to ring one half beat before beginning the SL. Allow the SL-notes to sound for one half beat before plucking the next M-note.

An arrangement of that old favorite "Cripple Creek" will give you some slide practice. Note that Roman numerals indicating position have been inserted above the staff for the first time. Review the paragraph on Fingering in the previous chapter before going on.

Cripple Creek

Double Thumbing

One of the great advances in clawhammer style was the discovery that the thumb could also be used to pluck the long strings of the banjo. Below is an exercise designed to teach this technique, known as *double thumbing* or *drop thumbing*.

Double Thumbing Exercise

In the first measure above, make sure that your hand is placed so that each time M plucks the first string, T is sitting on the fifth string, ready to play.

Keep practicing this measure until you can perform this maneuver consistently. In the next measure, you must place your hand so that each time M plucks the second string, T is sitting on the fifth string, ready to play. By the time M is plucking the fourth string (with T sitting on the fifth string, ready to play) you have achieved the spacing between M and T necessary for double thumbing. Without changing that spacing, move your entire hand over to the first string and try an M-T combination on strings 1 and 2. Then try drop thumbing on the other strings. Make sure all your M's and T's are exactly even.

Below is an old minstrel show tune called "Boatman," written in the mid-1800s by Dan Emmett, the best known stroke style player of them all. The tune is arranged with some first- and second-string double thumbing.

Boatman

Tuning: g DGBD

By Dan Emmett

Track 5

The Quick Slide

A *quick slide* (qSL) is best thought of as a decoration on the target note (see discussion on SL's). When performing a qSL, start moving toward the target fret the very instant the M-note is plucked. In fact, your finger should leave the M-note fret so rapidly that the M-note is barely perceived. To show just how short the M-note of a qSL operation is, I've notated it as a grace note, which (as you know) is considered to have virtually no duration. As can be seen below, the target note can be either an eighth note or a quarter note.

MqSL   MqSL   T

"Georgia Railroad," recorded in the 1920s by Gid Tanner and the Skillet Lickers, has been arranged with some qSL's and also with some drop thumbing on the second-to-third and third-to-fourth strings.

Georgia Railroad

Tuning: g DGBD

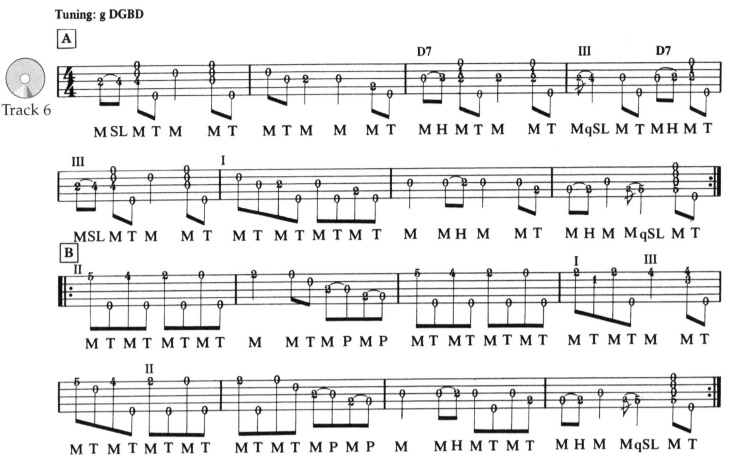

Track 6

Modes

The eight-note major scale (*do re mi fa so la ti do*) has been around only since the sixteenth century. Many traditional tunes have their roots in a more distant past, however, and their notes are organized in what are called *church modes*. These modes, which were originally used for the singing of Gregorian chants, involve different starting and ending points for the eight notes. The following modes will be found in this book:

The **Dorian** mode starts and ends on *re* (*re mi fa so la ti do re*). It has a sad, plaintive quality and is the mode most often played out of mountain minor tuning. ("Shady Grove" is in the Dorian mode.) Dorian tunes have guitar chord accompaniments such as Am-D-G, Dm-G-C, or Em-A-D.

The **Mixolydian** (mix-oh-lih-dee-an) mode runs from *so* to *so* (*so la ti do re mi fa so*). It sounds like a major scale in which the seventh note has been lowered in pitch by one half tone (one fret on the banjo). Mixolydian tunes ("Old Joe Clarke," for example) have guitar chord accompaniments such as G-C-F, D-G-C, and C-F-Bb .

The **Aeolian** (ay-oh-lee-an) mode runs from *la* to *la* (*la ti do re mi fa so la*). It is also called *natural minor* because sixteenth-century musicians derived what is now called the minor scale from the Aeolian mode by raising the pitch of its seventh note one half tone. Minor tunes (rare in traditional music) have guitar chord accompaniments of Am-Dm-E and Em-Am-B. Aeolian tunes ("The Rights of Man," for example) have accompaniments of Am-Dm-G and Em-Am-D.

Further Techniques

This chapter has covered the basic skills that go into melodic clawhammering. More advanced techniques will be introduced as needed. The list below shows where each of these techniques is discussed:

String Band Tunes

These tunes either derive from, or are strongly associated with the American South. Although each region - the Appalachians, the Southeast, eastern Texas and the Ozarks - had its own distinct fiddling style, overall the music played throughout the South had much in common. Most of the tunes in this chapter came to the attention of the contemporary old-time music scene via one of three sources - commercial country-music recordings from the 1920s and 30s (sometimes referred to as "hillbilly" recordings), Library of Congress field recordings from the 1930s and 40s, or the activities of independent collectors in the 1960s.

Most of the dance tunes recorded were in 4/4 time and ordinarily consisted of two eight measure sections played twice through (the A part and the B part). As most musicians play them today, they often feature a strong insistent back beat. The so called back beat is also an important feature of blues, jazz, show tunes and, of course, rock and roll. There was a hit song that went "Rock and Roll music; any old way you choose it. It has a back beat you can't lose it. " These lyrics were trying to say that the rhythm of rock and roll is easy to follow because on the second and fourth beats of each measure of a rock and roll song the drummer steps on his bass drum pedal and bangs his sticks on the snare drum like so:

one TWO three FOUR

To give you a better idea of what this is all about, below is printed the first two measures of "The Ways of the World." Emphasized notes are marked with an asterisk.

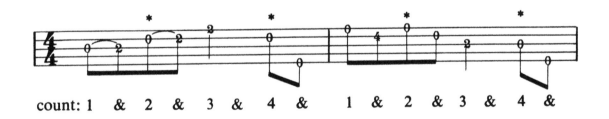

The fact that a measure is played with a back beat does not change the location of the melodic accent. In other words, when learning a tune from tablature, continue to emphasize the first beat, counting: 1&2&3&4&. Then, when you have become familiar with the melody, begin playing the tune with a back beat: 1&2&3&4&.

The Ways of the World

Key: C Major
(Fiddler plays in D: capo-2)

This is an Appalachian tune first recorded in 1937 by fiddler Luther Strong of Dalesbury, KY. It can be heard on *Fire on the Mountain: The High Woods String Band* (Rounder 0023) and also on *Allan Block and Ralph Lee Smith* (Meadowlands MS1). The B part does not repeat.

Tuning: g CGCD

Track 7

Sandy River Belle

Key: G Major
(Fiddler plays in A: capo-2)

This tune comes from the area surrounding Meadows of Dan, VA where to this day banjo pickers play it in a special Sandy River Belle tuning (gDGDE). It was originally recorded in 1927 by Dad Blackard's Moonshiners. A very sweet banjo and hammered dulcimer version can be heard on *Sarah Grey with Ed Trickett* (Folk Legacy FSI-38).

Tuning: g DGBD

Track 8

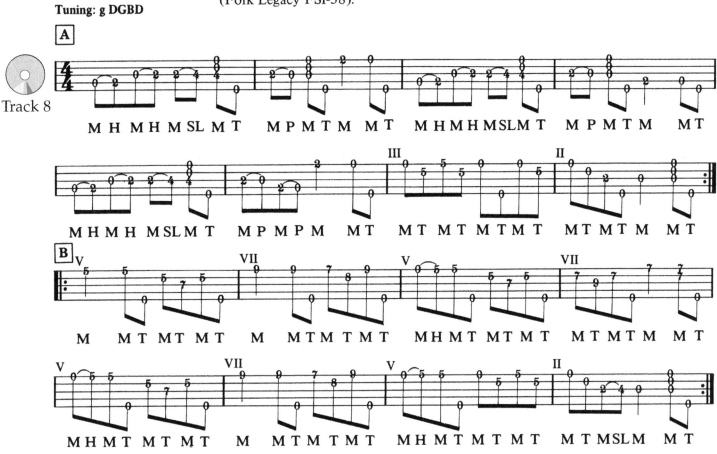

25

Old Mother Flanagan

Key: G Major
(Fiddler plays in A: capo-2)

The Fuzzy Mountain String Band (Rounder 0010) collected this tune from Lee Triplett of Clay County, VA. The B part is closely related to that of an Irish reel called "The Green Fields of America."

Track 9

Tuning: g DGBD

Dotted Quarter Notes

A dot added to any note increases its value by 50%. A dotted quarter note, then, is held for 1½ beats before the next note is plucked. In part A, measure 6 of "Dry and Dusty" there's a dotted quarter followed by an eighth note. Make sure you count "3 & 4" before beginning your pull-off.

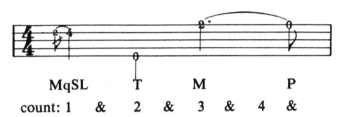

	MqSL		T		M		P	
count:	1	&	2	&	3	&	4	&

Quarter Notes on the Fifth String

If you look again at the above measure, you'll notice that the T-note on the fifth string is a quarter note. Make sure you allow it to ring for a full beat before plucking the next M-note.

Dry and Dusty

Key: C Major
(Fiddler plays in D: capo-2)

Whenever an Ozark fiddler wanted a drink at a square dance he played this tune to let his audience know that he was "Dry and Dusty." A 1930 version by the Morrison Twin Brothers String Band of Arkansas can be heard on an anthology called *Echoes of the Ozarks* (County 518).

Tuning: g CGCD

Track 10

27

Alternate String Pull-Offs

Here M strikes one string (either fretted or unfretted) and a finger of the fretting hand pulls-off *another* string. To get a continuous sound, the finger being used to pull-off the alternate string must be down on that string when the M-note is plucked. Both the M-note and the alternate string P-note should be exactly even.

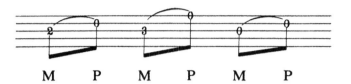

M plucks 3rd string

1st finger pulls off 2nd string

Frosty Morning

Alan Jabbour collected this one from West Virginia fiddler Henry Reed, who was also the source for many other tunes now popular among old timey musicians. "Frosty Morning" can be heard on *The Fuzzy Mountain String Band* (Rounder 0010).

Tuning: g DGCD

Track 11

The Eighth of January

Key: C Major
(Fiddler plays in D: capo-2)

On January 8, 1815, American forces under Andrew Jackson defeated the British at New Orleans. Originally called "Jackson's Victory," this tune was renamed when Jackson fell from popular favor around the time of the Civil War. In the 1950s, Jimmy Driftwood wrote a set of lyrics to this melody, called "The Battle of New Orleans."

Tuning: g CGCD

Track 12

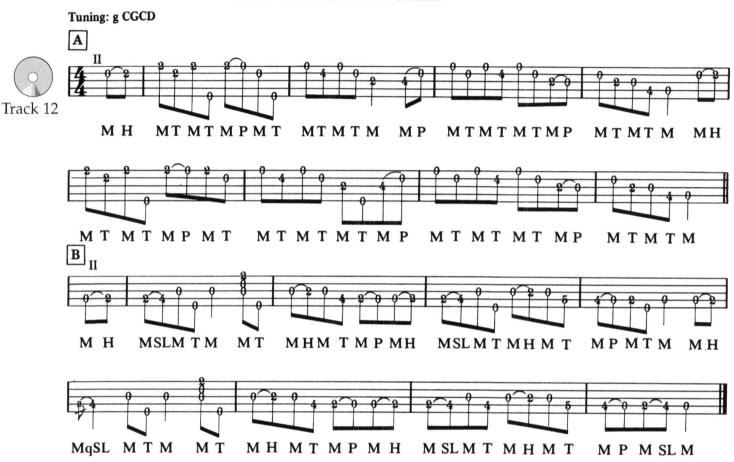

The Triplet

A triplet is a group of three, even notes played in the space of one beat. Each note in a triplet grouping takes up exactly 1/3 beat. Let's look at a $\frac{4}{4}$ measure made up entirely of triplets.

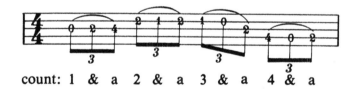

count: 1 & a 2 & a 3 & a 4 & a

When, as is often the case in fiddle music, eighth-note pairs and triplets occur in the same measure, you have to learn to divide beats alternately into two's (1&2&) and three's (1&a2&a) without allowing the pace of the tune to falter. In part B, measure 6 of "Jubilo" we have the following:

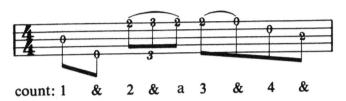

count: 1   &   2   &   a   3   &   4   &

Here the first, third, and fourth beats are divided into two parts, while the second beat is divided into three parts. The second beat (containing three notes) takes up no more time than any of the other beats (containing only two notes). *The basic pulse of a tune must remain constant no matter what sort of notes (eighths, quarters, triplets) are present in the melody line.*

In clawhammer style, the first note of a triplet is usually played by M, while the second and third notes are ordinarily obtained by exactly timed combinations of H's and P's.

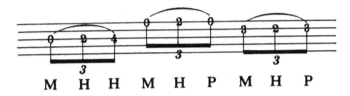

M   H   H   M   H   P   M   H   P

Substituting an H or P for a Drone Note

Here M brushes across several strings, but instead of striking the fifth string we get a sound similar to that of a bum-titty strum by performing an H or P on one of the brushed strings.

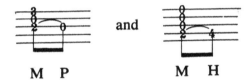

M   P   and   M   H

The Year of Jubilo

Key: C Major
(Fiddler plays in D: capo-2)

This is the tune that's always heard in the background of old Civil War movies. A minstrel show song written in 1872 by Henry C. Work, its comic lyrics tell of events on the plantation after Lincoln's proclamation ended slavery in that "year of Jubilo," 1864. (A Jubilee Year, during which all slaves were freed, was declared every half century by the ancient Hebrews.) On *Stolen Love: The Red Clay Ramblers* (Flying Fish FF009).

Tuning: g CGCD

By Henry C. Work

Track 13

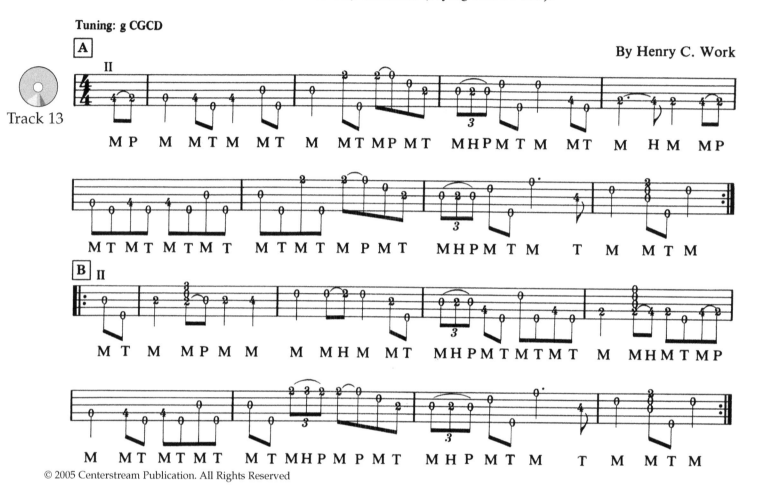

Bob Carlin

Bob Carlin organized and performed on the Kicking Mule *Melodic Clawhammer Banjo* album (KM 209). Originally a guitarist, he learned melodic clawhammering from Hank Sapoznik. (Both are members of the Delaware Water Gap String Band.) Bob's current playing is a blend of Hank's strictly melodic approach with the more driving string band style of Round Peak, NC clawhammerer Fred Cockerham. Nowadays, Carlin produces banjo and other old timey records for Kicking Mule and hosts "Dance All Night," a Philadelphia radio show on WUHY-FM that is devoted to old timey and bluegrass music.

Jimmy in the Swamp

Keys: Part A: F Major
      Part B: D Aeolian
(Fiddler plays in G &
 E: capo-2)

Robert Christeson, author of *The Old Time Fiddler's Repertory,* got this tune from Nebraska fiddler Uncle Bob Walters. Bob Carlin learned it from Pete Southerland of Vermont's Arm and Hammer String Band. Note that in the first and fifth measures of part B, Bob strikes one string and hammers-down on two strings.

Tuning: fCFCD

Arranged by Bob Carlin

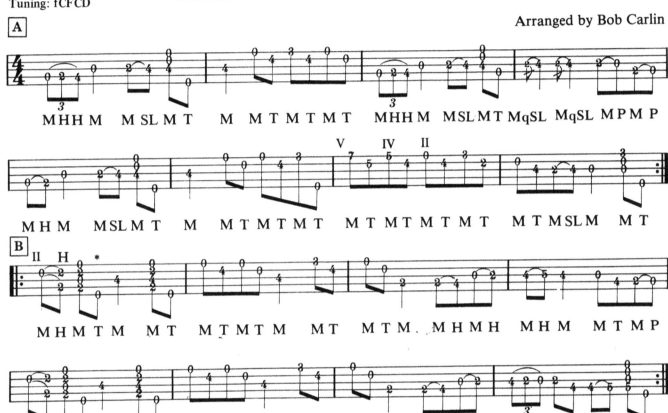

Track 14

33

The West Fork Gals

This West Virginia tune can be heard on *Summer Oaks and Porch: The Fuzzy Mountain String Band* (Rounder 0035). It may be related to an Irish reel called "The Wexford Lasses" (see *O'Neill's Music of Ireland).*

Tuning: g CGCD

Track 15

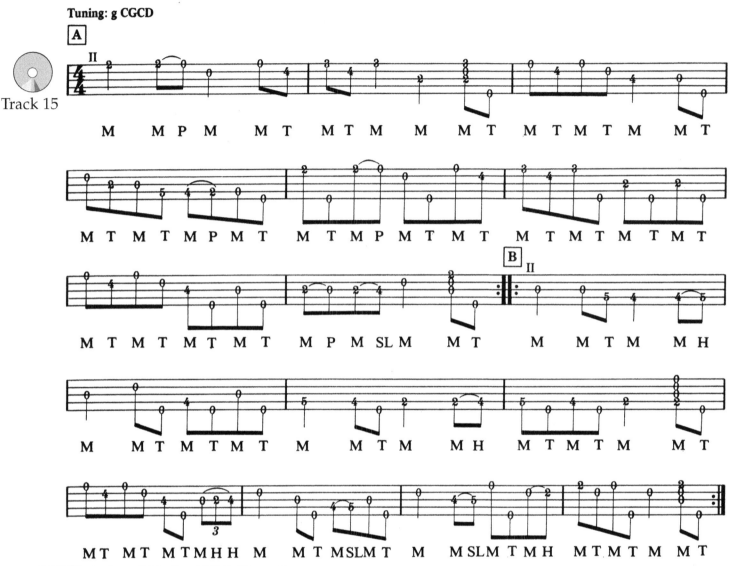

© 2005 Centerstream Publication. All Rights Reserved

Alternate String Hammer-Ons

Here one string (fretted or unfretted) is struck by M, and a finger of the fretting hand hammers-on to another string. The M-note and the alternate string H-note should be exactly even.

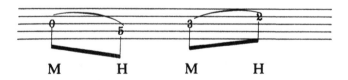

As can be seen above, the H-note of an alternate string hammer-on can occur on a string higher or lower than the M-note string.

Obtaining Triplets with M-P-T Combinations

This is a technique Howie frequently uses in his playing. So far we've obtained the second and third notes of triplets with combinations of H's and P's. However, sometimes the third note of a triplet can be plucked by T, yielding figures like this:

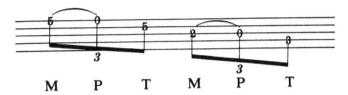

M   P   T   M   P   T

These M-P-T triplets are essentially an ordinary M-T combination with a pull-off inserted between the M-note and the T-note. Each note should be allowed to ring exactly 1/3 beat.

Howie Bursen

Howie was the first truly melodic clawhammerer I encountered, and his approach to the banjo greatly influenced my playing style. He introduced me to the melodic possibilities of alternate string H's and P's, convinced me that clawhammering could be a beautiful and intricate form of banjo playing, and encouraged my first efforts in melodic arranging. In the last few years, Howie has developed a style in which he plays each repetition of a fiddle tune with more and more elaboration. He is particularly fond of the triplet as a means of ornamenting his tunes, and he uses this technique to perfection. An excellent guitarist and superb singer as well, Howie has recently recorded an album for Folk Legacy Records.

Salt River

Key: G Mixolydian
(Fiddler plays in A: capo-2)

Howie learned this tune from John Roberts, an English singer and banjo player now residing in Marlboro, VT. It is most likely the ancestor of that bluegrass favorite "Salt Creek." The first time through, Howie plays a basic version of the tune. The variation shows his method for elaborating on a simple melody.

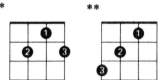

Tuning: g DGBD

Track 16

Arranged by Howie Bursen

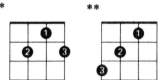

36

B

MT MPTMTMTMT MPTMTMTMT MPPMTMTMT MPPMTMTMT

MPTMTMTMT MPTMTMTMT MPPMTM·TMSL M MTM MT

The Roll

A *roll* is a slow, controlled brush. M starts on the fourth string and, without lifting off the strings, it proceeds to pluck the third, second, and first strings; then the fifth string is struck by T. The whole process takes a little more than one beat. In order to get the right sound, M must dwell on each string exactly the same amount of time, and there must be no perceivable break between the plucking of the first string by M and the plucking of the fifth string by T. If a roll were written out, it would look like this:

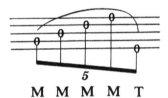

M M M M T

But it is usually notated like this:

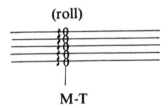

(roll)

M-T

37

Kitchen Girl

This is another tune collected from West Virginia fiddler Henry Reed. It can be heard on *The Hollow Rock String Band* (Kanawha 311). It's one of my favorites!

Tuning: g DGCD

Hank Sapoznik

Hank learned basic clawhammer style from Bill Garbus of New York, NY, and studied briefly with Fred Cockerham. Others who influenced his playing were Blanton Owen (of the Fuzzy Mountain String Band) and Art Rosenbaum (author of *Old Time Mountain Banjo).* Hank now plays a thoroughly melodic style, as he does not feel that he has to be "limited by the role the banjo once played as a backup instrument." He tends to use drop thumbing whenever possible because he feels this gives the banjo a cleaner, more projecting sound. His playing can be heard on *Melodic Clawhammer Banjo* (Kicking Mule 209) and also as backup on *Sweeney's Dream: Kevin Burke Plays Traditional Dance Tunes from Sligo Ireland* (F&W 8876). Besides clawhammering, Hank also plays some classical banjo and is now producing an album on the subject for Kicking Mule. He plays banjo in the Delaware Water Gap String Band (listen to Adelphi 2004), and his tabs often appear in *Sing Out!* and *Banjo News-letter.*

Hedy West

M-Skipping

In "Avalon Quickstep" there is the following figure:

There are two ways of approaching this:
1) Treat it as an ordinary dotted quarter and eighth-note combination. In other words, wait 1½ beats after M strikes fret 2, first string, before using T on the fifth string.
2) Play the passage as if it were written as follows, making a motion to strike one of the strings with M at beat 3 but not actually doing so.

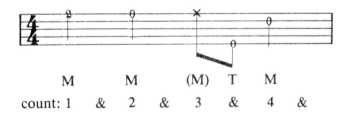

This procedure, which I'll call *M-skipping*, gives a nice, percussive sound to the fifth string that fits in well with many string band tunes.

The Avalon Quickstep

Key: C Major
(Fiddler plays in D: capo-2)

Named for Avalon, Mississippi, this tune was recorded in 1929 by W.T. Namour and S.W. Smith (on *The Traditional Music of Mississippi*, County 528). Both part A (measure 6) and part B (measure 5) contain quarter rests, so make sure that a full beat is left open at these points. Note that part B has ten measures instead of the usual eight.

Tuning: g CGCD

Arranged by Hank Sapoznik

Track 18

Syncopation

Syncopation can be defined as playing between the beats a note that the ear is expecting to hear on the beat. Syncopated passages are difficult to notate and read, so I'll suggest an easy method for dealing with them.

"Colored Aristocracy" contains the following syncopated measure (part A, measure 7, second ending). It is syncopated because the open first-string note falls between the second and third beats, instead of directly on beat 3.

Syncopated measure

count: 1   &   2   &   3   &   4   &

Same measure, unsyncopated

count: 1   &   2   &   3   &   4   &

To get the feel for this measure, count out the beats, leaving a full half-beat space at count 3, where the eighth rest occurs. If this is not sufficient, try actually dividing the measure up into eight equal spaces (one for each half beat) and note how the space above count 3 is empty. This should help you visualize exactly how long each note should sound in a syncopated passage.

count: 1   &   2   &   3   &   4   &

Colored Aristocracy

Key: G Major

Composed in the late nineteenth century, "Colored Aristocracy" is technically a cakewalk rather than a true fiddle tune. (Cakewalks were the slightly syncopated ancestors of ragtime.) Taj Mahal plays an interesting clawhammer version on *De Old Folks at Home* (Columbia GP18).

Tuning: g DGBD

Track 19

Eric Mintz

I've known Eric since our first day at Cornell University (Ithaca, NY). He was playing his Vega Whyte Ladye #2 outside the freshman dorms, and I couldn't resist running over to make his acquaintance. He was into Seeger-style frailing at the time, but over the years, under the influence of such Ithaca claw-hammerers as Walt Koken and Howie Bursen, his playing has become more and more melodic. Nowadays, Eric (who also plays concertina) is particularly interested in English traditional music, and also in highly syncopated Southern tunes like "Clinch Mountain Backstep." He has recently developed a *thumb-over* technique in which T actually crosses over M to play a higher string during a drop thumb operation. His style reflects his belief that "the banjo is an instrument that should be played sweetly and softly."

Playing "Short Measures"

Part B, measure 5 of "The Clinch Mountain Backstep" has only two beats. Don't let this throw you. Just remember the following about *short measures,* which are fairly common in Southern fiddle music:

— The first beat of a short measure is accented in the same way as the first beat of a measure of normal length.

— Each beat in a short measure has the same duration as any of the beats contained in the normal-length measures of a tune.

So if we have a short measure surrounded by two normal-length measures, the count is as follows:

ONE two three four|ONE two|ONE two three four

More M-Skipping

"Clinch Mountain Backstep" contains the following figures which can be handled as follows:

Part A, measure 4

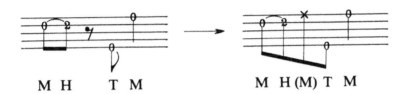

M H   T M   M H (M) T M

Part B, measure 3

M SL   T M   M SL (M) T M

Part B, measure 8

M T   T M T   M T (M) T M T

The Clinch Mountain Backstep

Eric learned this one from Walt Koken, who is best known as the fiddler and front man for Ithaca's Highwoods String Band (listen to Rounder 0023). Ralph Stanley recorded the tune in clawhammer style back in the 1930s, but his later Scruggs-picking version is much better known. The arrangement below shows off Eric's ability to bring out difficult syncopated lines with a minimum of left-hand work. (Note that T *precedes* M on the fourth beat of bars 1 and 5 in part A and bar 6 of part B.)

Tuning: g DGCD

Track 20

Arranged by Eric Mintz

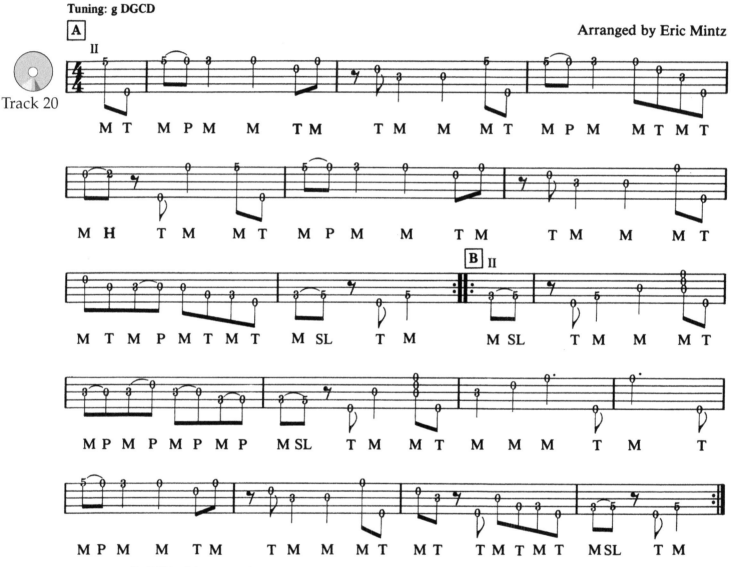

Fretting the Fifth String

Somewhere along the line, somebody decided that fretting the fifth string of a banjo was a big production. Some players still think it's pretty weird. I think it's the most natural thing in the world, but fingering diagrams will be provided whenever the drone string is to be fretted. Be sure to reread the section on fifth string notation before you proceed.

When a capo is used, raising the pitch of the long strings of the banjo, some means must be found to raise the pitch of the fifth string by the same amount. I've always used a "railroad spike" or fifth-string capo for this purpose, but if you actually retune the fifth string, remember that the frets at which certain pitches can be obtained will change. In other words, if you tune your fifth string up two frets to match a long-string capo at the second fret, you must subtract 2 from each fifth-string notation.

The Cherokee Shuffle

Key: G Major
(Fiddler plays in A: capo-2)

This old timey favorite is closely related to a tune in D Major called "Lost Indian." It can be heard on *String Band Music: The Delaware Water Gap String Band* (Adelphi AD 2004). Note that the B part is ten measures in length.

Tuning: g DGBD

Track 21

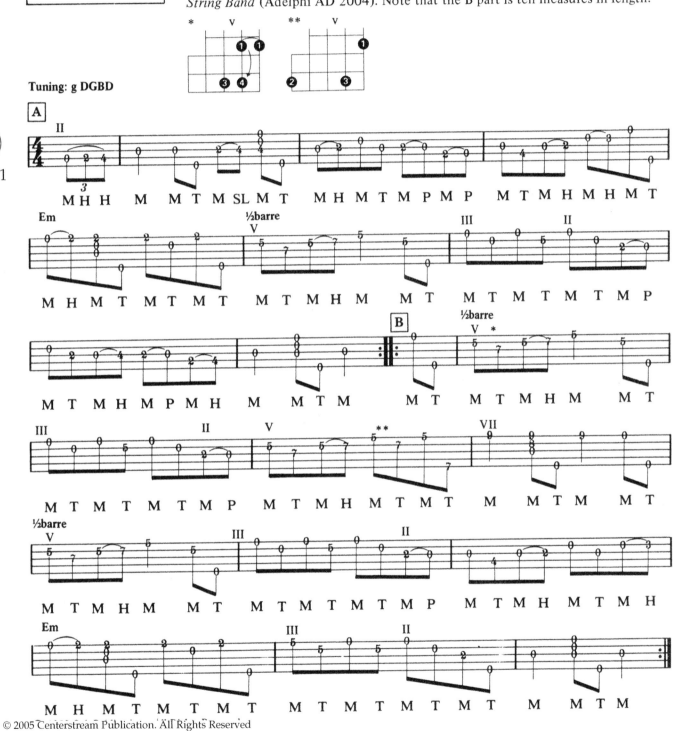

47

Double Stops

Old timey and bluegrass fiddlers often bow and "fret" two strings at once. This technique is called *double stopping*. As you know, hitting two strings at the same time on the banjo presents no particular problem, but being able to control exactly which two (or three) strings are struck requires some practice. In "Ragtime Annie" some passages in parts B and C call for double stops on strings 3 and 4. Special care must be taken to avoid hitting any but these strings.

Ragtime Annie

Keys: Parts A and B: C Major
Part C: F Major
(Fiddler plays in D and
G: capo-2)

As the title suggests, this highly syncopated fiddle tune is heavily influenced by a form of music called ragtime. Rags were made up of three or four sixteen-measure parts (note the length of "Annie's" B part). The C part (like "Annie's") was usually in a different key from the other parts. For a special treat, listen to Doc Watson's brilliant flatpick-guitar version of "Ragtime Annie" (Vanguard VSD 79170, *Doc Watson and Son)*. The arrangement below is based on a recording by fiddler Clark Kessinger (*Old Time Fiddle Classics,* County 507).

Blackberry Blossom

Key: G Major

Originally recorded in 1929 by the Arthur Smith Trio, this tune has become a favorite among bluegrassers. A version by Sonny Miller and the Southern Mountain Boys can be heard on *Virginia Breakdown* (County 705).

Tuning: g DGBD

Track 23

Whiskey Before Breakfast

Key: C Major
(Fiddler plays in D: capo-2)

I learned "Whiskey Before Breakfast" from Ithaca fiddler Nick Krukovsky. The tune comes from Canada's maritime provinces where they call it "The Spirits of the Morning." Despite its alien origin, "Whiskey" has become extremely popular among old timey musicians in the last few years, and it is the title cut of a recent album by The Arkansas Sheiks (Bay 204). A finger-style guitar version of this tune appears in *Fingerpicking Fiddle Tunes.* The arrangement below includes an up-the-neck variation on the B part of "Whiskey."

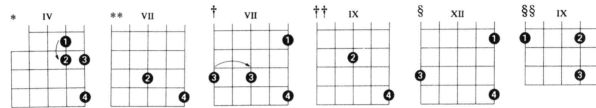

Tuning: g CGCD

Track 24

A

MH MHM MH M T M T M MT M MT M MT MT M T MT MT MT M P

MHMHMT MH MT MT M MT MTMT MT MT MT MHM MT

B

MqSL MTM MH MTMTMP MP M MTM MT MTMTMP MH

M MT M MT MP MP MPMP M MTMTMT MP M SLM MT

B Variation

½ barre

MqSL MTM MT MTMTMT MT MqSL MTM MT MTMT MTMT

M MTM MT MT MT MTMT MTMT MTM MTMHM MT

Jigs, Reels, Hornpipes and Set Tunes

For the most part, these tunes hale from eighteenth- and nineteenth-century Ireland, England, and Scotland. They were composed as accompaniments for two broad categories of folk dance: step dancing and set dancing. Hornpipes were designed to accompany step dancing. Also called clogging, this is a solo form in which the dancer performs complicated maneuvers with his legs and feet, while holding his arms and torso nearly immobile. Reels and set tunes were designed to be played for set dancing, a type of social dance in which all figures are performed within each of several small groups or sets. (Both square and contra dancing are forms of set dance.) Jigs were originally step-dance tunes, but nowadays they are also used in many regions for accompanying set dances.

American fiddle tunes are directly descended from these old world dance tunes. Almost the entire New England fiddling repertoire comes from published collections of British, Irish, and Scottish tunes; and even most native New England tunes stick very closely to old world patterns. String band music is descended from the playing of the Scottish and Irish fiddlers who settled in remote parts of the South in the years 1750-1825. Although fiddling styles have changed considerably in these areas since that time, many old world tunes are still played, and the structure of most home grown tunes is not fundamentally different from that of tunes brought from Britain and Ireland nearly two centuries ago.

Jigs, reels, hornpipes, and set tunes are usually made up of two eight-measure sections played twice through. They tend to have fairly complex and tuneful melodies which are often modal instead of major or minor. Unlike the string band tunes, which (being in $\frac{4}{4}$ time) have four beats per measure with the accent on the second and fourth, old world tunes tend to have two beats per measure with an accent on each beat. Jigs are written in $\frac{6}{8}$ time (see p. 78), while set tunes, hornpipes, and reels are played in what is known as *cut time*.

Playing in Cut Time

Let's look at a measure from "The Cherokee Shuffle" which, when played in string band style, contains four beats, or one beginning every other eighth note.

* — primary accent
> — secondary accent

sounds like: da – da,   Da – da,   da – da,   Da – da

If a New England or Irish fiddler approached this same measure, he would play it with only *two* beats, or one beginning every fourth eighth note. The tempo (rate of speed) within the measure remains the same as before.

sounds like: Da – da – da – da, Da – da – da – da

When the number of beats in a measure of four quarter notes is halved in this manner, it is called *cut time* and the time signature is $\frac{2}{2}$ or ¢ .

Phrasing

Musical notes are not usually played exactly as written. They are grouped or *phrased* in a particular manner, depending on the character of a tune. Traditional dance tunes tend to have very consistent phrasing, because dancers need secure, predictable musical patterns in order to feel free to absorb themselves in dance movements. The phrases of jigs, reels, hornpipes, and set tunes are built around the strongest beat of each measure (downbeat). Phrases begin on the upbeat (the note that *precedes* this strongest beat) and run to a point just before the next upbeat. Because upbeats are used by musicians as a means to lean into the downbeats of the following measures I've called them *pivot notes.*

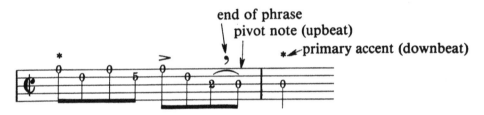

sounds like: Da–da –da–da, Da–da–da–da – Da

Set Tunes

Called polkas in Ireland, set tunes are the simplest cut-time fiddle tunes. They are based on a structure of four quarter notes per measure with accents on the first and third. Any quarter note can be replaced by two eighth notes, but usually no more than two such substitutions occur per measure.

sounds like: Dot–dot–Dot–dot   Dot–da da Da-da-dot

On the banjo, set tunes usually need some fleshing out in order to sound interesting. This is done by frequently inserting drone notes between quarter notes, and by occasionally replacing a quarter-note passage with an eighth-note run. Polkas are light-hearted tunes that should be played at a moderate pace with an almost bouncy feel.

In a typical set tune, the phrase begins at the last quarter note (upbeat) of a measure. This pivot note is used to lean into the downbeat of the next measure. The phrase continues until just before the next pivot note and is followed by an almost imperceptible pause. A new phrase then begins at the new pivot note. So, although a set tune is written:

Tuning: g CGCD

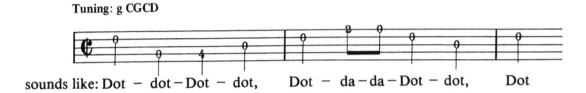

sounds like: Dot — dot — Dot — dot,   Dot — da — da — Dot — dot,   Dot

The actual sound is:

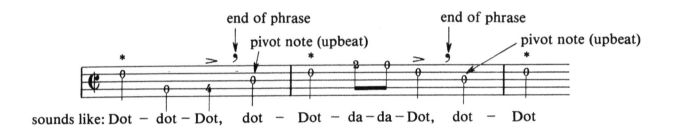

sounds like: Dot — dot — Dot,   dot — Dot — da — da — Dot,   dot — Dot

Campbell's Farewell to Redgap

Key: G Mixolydian
(Fiddler plays in A: capo-2)

I learned this one from Ron Osborne, a North Carolina guitarist and mandolin player now living in New York. The title is intriguing and I'm sure there's an interesting story behind the tune, but I haven't been able to locate anyone who knows it. I would guess that the tune is Scottish—both from its title and from its use of the A Mixolydian mode. It can be heard on *Kenny Hall* (Philo 1008).

Tuning: g DGBD

Ornamentation

Players of traditional fiddle music like to ornament or embellish important notes of a tune by adding to them one or more quick notes. Each national and regional style has its own rules concerning what sort of ornaments can be used, where they can be inserted, and how often they can appear in a given tune section. Types of ornaments include:

The Ornamental Triplet. Here a quarter note or an eighth-note pair is replaced by a triplet. This triplet is made up of pitches originally found in the tune plus one or two adjacent notes.

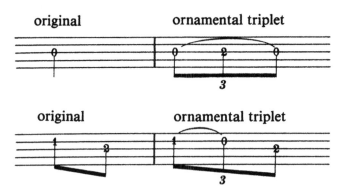

French Canadian fiddlers are noted for their constant use of ornamental triplets, while New Englanders tend to throw in maybe one or two per tune. Irish musicians use them mainly in hornpipes. On the banjo, Howie Bursen's variations on "Salt River" and "The Linnet" demonstrate tasteful use of this ornamenting technique.

The Grace Note You've seen this symbol in connection with qSL's. A grace note is an exceptionally quick note that is considered to have no time value of its own. Instead it borrows a tiny length of time from the note which follows it. On the banjo, grace notes are usually obtained by a very rapid pull-off. This P should be so quick that the M-note is barely perceived.

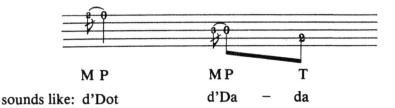

Grace notes are used primarily by Irish fiddlers to ornament jigs and reels.

The Double Grace Note  This is a group of two rapid, even notes, considered to have no time value of their own. Each is about the length of a single grace note, and each borrows a tiny amount of time from the note which follows them. On the banjo, double grace notes are obtained by extremely rapid combinations of H's and P's.

M P H   M H P   P

sounds like: d'd'Dot   d'd'Da — da

The double grace note is used very frequently (in all types of tunes) by Irish fiddlers and occasionally by British and New England fiddlers.

The Irish Roll. These four- and five-note ornaments are extremely difficult on the banjo because the instrument often won't sustain long enough to allow for a sequence of so many H's and P's. An Irish roll, notated for banjo, appears as follows:

Tuning: g CGCD

5-note roll

M   H P P H   T

Andy McGann and Paddy Reynolds

57

57

Nancy

Key: C Major
(Fiddler plays in D: capo-2)

This tune was written in the 1920s by piper Tom Clough of Northumberland, a region in the northeast corner of England. It's been one of my favorite tunes ever since Howie Bursen taught it to me some years ago. "Nancy" is printed in the *Northumbrian Piper's Tune Book* and can be heard on *Northumbria Forever: The High Level Ranters* (Trailer 2007). A finger-style guitar version appears in *Fingerpicking Fiddle Tunes*.

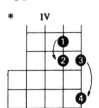

Tuning: g CGCD

By Tom Clough

Track 26

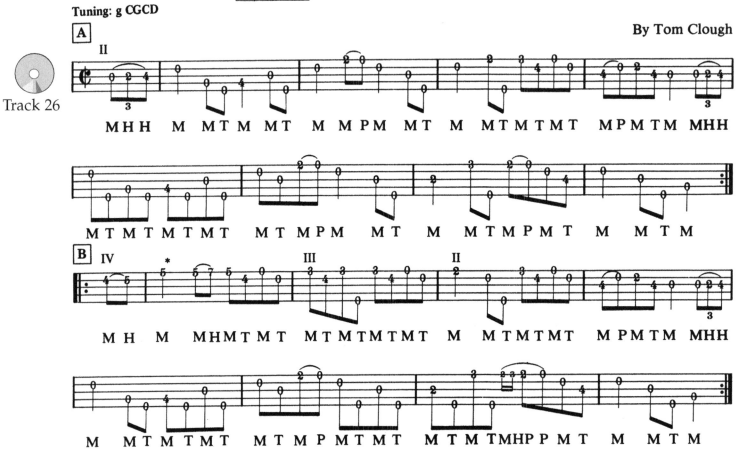

A Farewell to Whiskey

Key: G Major

Neil Gow (pronounced "Go"), an eighteenth century Scottish fiddler, wrote this tune to lament an English ban on whiskey manufacturing in Scotland. Originally a slow, mournful aire, something in the tune's character has led successive generations of fiddlers to quicken its tempo and lighten its mood. It is now played as a spirited set tune in Scotland, Ireland, and New England. On *The Star above the Garter: Dennis Murphy* (Claddagh CC5).

Tuning: g DGBD

By Neil Gow

Track 27

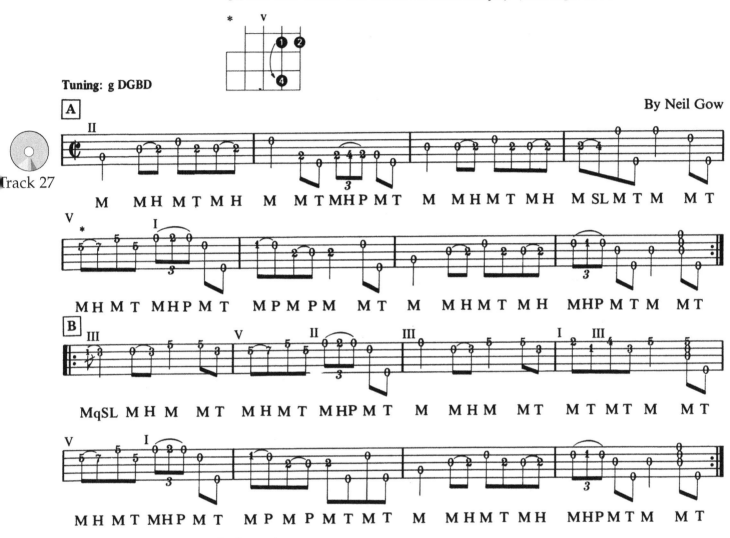

Petronella

This Scottish tune is used extensively in New England for accompanying contra dances. I learned it from fiddler Colin Quigley of Chappaqua, NY.

Tuning: g CGCD

Track 28

Two Balleydesmond Polkas

These are two untitled tunes commonly played in the area surrounding the town of Balleydesmond, County Kerry, Ireland. (Kerry musicians, from whom most Irish polkas derive, are notorious for never naming them.) Printed in the *Armagh Piper's Club Tune Book,* these tunes can be heard on *Johnny Cronin and Joe Burke* (Shanachie 29005). And don't forget to check out the brilliant string-band-style version of "Balleydesmond" performed by the Red Clay Ramblers on an album called *Stolen Love* (Flying Fish FF009).

Tuning: g CGCD

Track 29

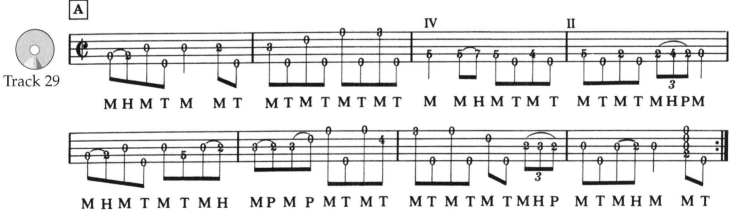

60

Tuning: g CGCD

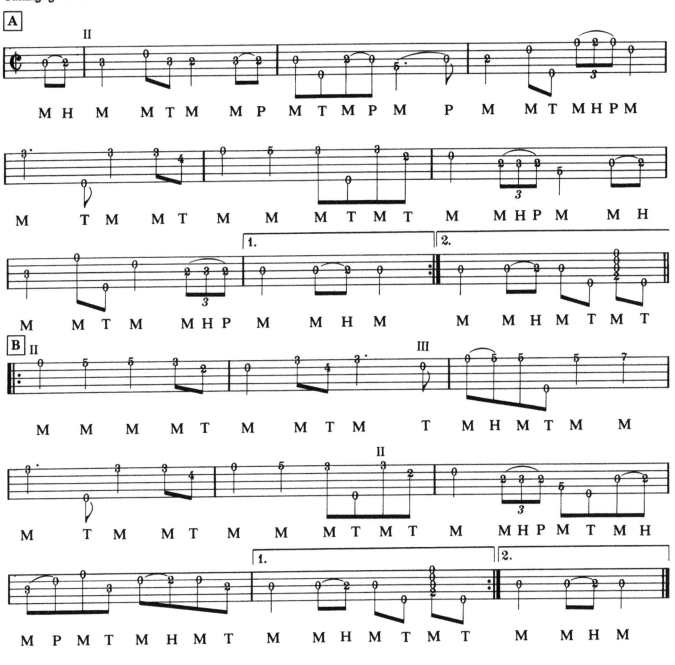

The Linnet

Keys: Part A: C Major
Part B: C Mixolydian
(Fiddler plays in D: capo-2)

The linnet is a small European songbird, sometimes used as a symbol for Napoleon in Irish folklore. I've included one of Howie's variations on the B part to demonstrate his extensive use of ornamental triplets.

Arranged by Howie Bursen

Tuning: g CGCD

Track 31

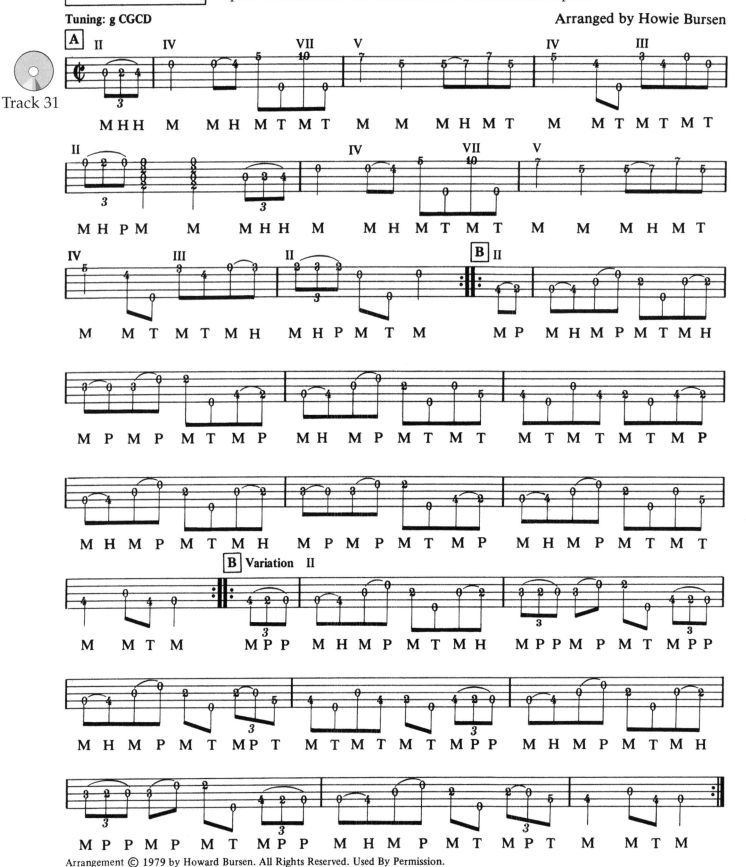

Hornpipes

Hornpipes are cut-time tunes based on a structure of eight eighth notes per measure, organized as two groups of four with an accent on the first note of each group. In most regions, these eighth notes are played as dotted pairs. In other words, the first and third notes of each group (dotted eighth notes) are allowed to sound substantially longer than the second and fourth notes (sixteenth notes). This yields the following:

sounds like: Dot — da — dot — da, Dot — da — dot — da

The last measure of each tune section ordinarily ends with three quarter notes.

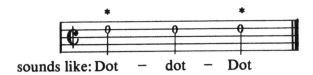

sounds like: Dot — dot — Dot

These tunes, written as accompaniment for step dances, had to be played at a slow to moderate tempo in order to give the dancer time to complete his maneuvers. Because hornpipes could not be played fast, special care was taken to give them interesting melodies, and many of the most memorable fiddle tunes played today are of this category.

Dotted hornpipes have two phrases per measure, centering around the two accented notes. Each phrase begins at the pivot note before each accented note, and continues to a point just before the next pivot note. So, although dotted hornpipes are written:

Tuning: g DGBD

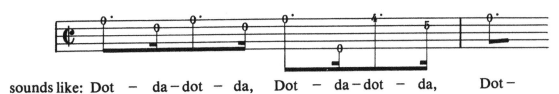

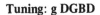
sounds like: Dot — da – dot — da, Dot — da – dot — da, Dot —

They are played:

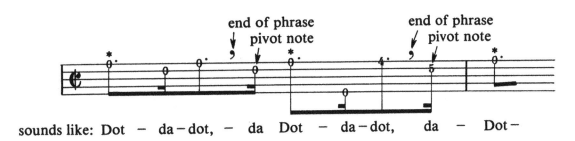

sounds like: Dot — da – dot, — da Dot — da – dot, da — Dot —

Hornpipes, New England Style

In New England, most hornpipes are played at a fairly quick tempo, without a dotted feel. They are then used to accompany set dances. For information on the phrasing of undotted hornpipes, see the discussion on reels, (p. 71).

The Lamplighter's Hornpipe

Key: G Major
(Fiddler plays in A: capo-2)

Hank learned this one from mandolinist John Jeffords of Belfast, Maine. It is printed in Cole's *One Thousand Fiddle Tunes*. Note how Hank frequently obtains runs of adjacent pitches by combining open-string M-notes, with up-the-neck T-notes.

Tuning: g DGBD

Arranged by Hank Sapoznik

Track 32

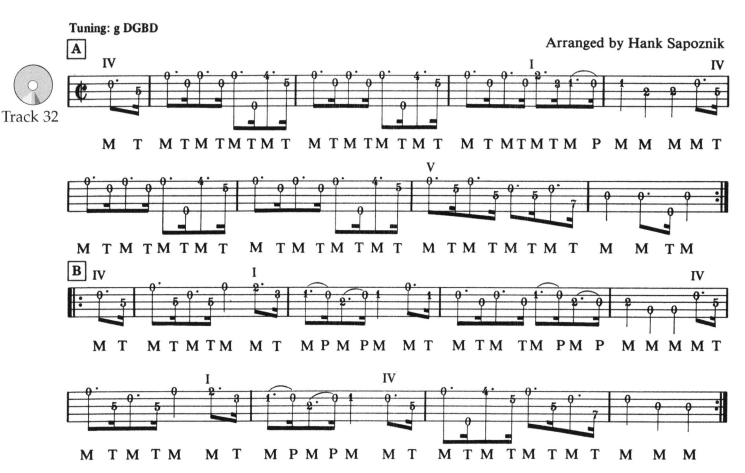

Old French

Keys: Part A: C Major
      Part B: G Mixolydian
(Fiddler plays in D and
A: capo-2)

This tune supposedly got its name from an old Vermont fiddler who declared, when asked its title, "Oh, it's just an old French tune." The fact is, "Old French" is virtually unknown in French Canada. It is, however, very popular in northern New England where it was probably composed as an attempt to imitate the sound of a typical Quebec dance tune. Also called "The Rambler's Hornpipe," it is printed in *The Nelson Collection* and can be heard on *Kenny Hall* (Philo 1008).

Tuning: g CGCD

Track 33

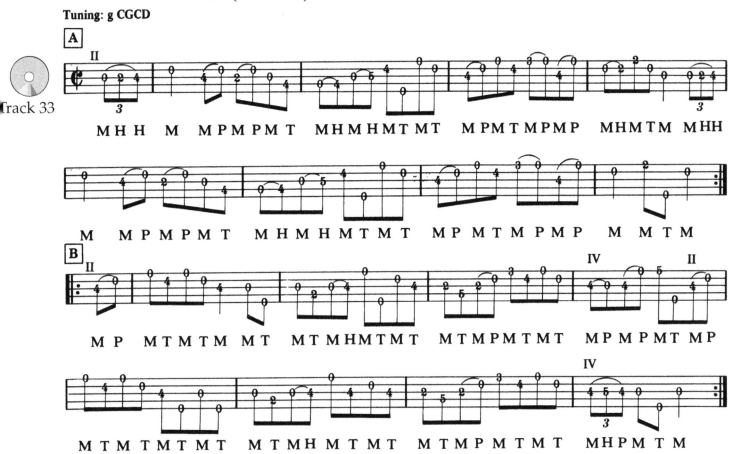

The Morpeth Rant

Key: C Major
(Fiddler plays in D: capo-2)

Morpeth (pronounced Mor'-peth) is a town in the Northumberland region of England where a dance has been done specifically to this tune for over a century and a half. "The Morpeth Rant" is printed in Cole's *One Thousand Fiddle Tunes* under the title "Morpeth's Hornpipe." It can be heard in New England style on *Allan Block and Ralph Lee Smith* (Meadowlands MS1). It can be played in either dotted or undotted rhythm.

Tuning: g CGCD

Clara's Hornpipe

Key: C Major
(Fiddler plays in D: capo-2)

Howie, who learned "Clara's Hornpipe" at a Vermont contra dance, describes it as his "current favorite tune." It is not structured like a conventional horn-pipe, so it may be a relatively recent New England tune, composed with no attempt to conform to old world tune categories.

Tuning: g CGCD

Arranged by Howie Bursen

Track 35

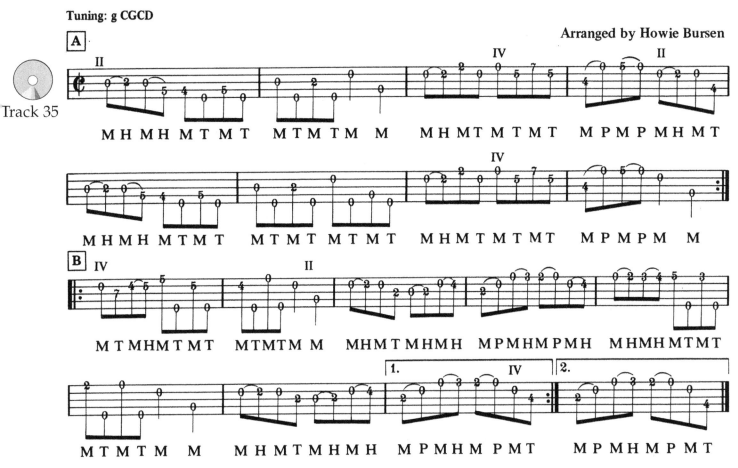

The Rights of Man

Key: E Aeolian

This haunting tune was probably written as a tribute to Tom Paine's famous eighteenth century pamphlet. It is printed in *Allen's Irish Fiddler* and can be heard on *The Hammered Dulcimer: Bill Spence and the Fennigs All Star Band* (Front Hall Records 01). A finger-style guitar arrangement of "The Rights of Man" appears in *Fingerpicking Fiddle Tunes.*

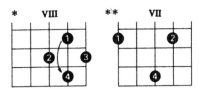

Tuning: g DGDB

Track 36

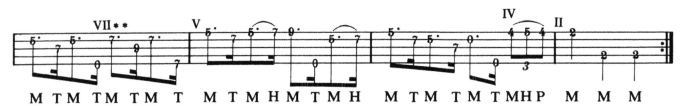

68

President Garfield's Hornpipe

Key: G Major
(Fiddler plays in Bb: capo-3)

James A. Garfield was elected twentieth president of the U.S. in 1880. He was assassinated shortly after taking office, but his name lives on in the title of this lovely New England tune. "President Garfield's Hornpipe" is printed in Cole's *One Thousand Fiddle Tunes* and can be heard on *No Curb Service Anymore: The Pine Island Band* (Green Mountain GMS 1052). Note that Hank tunes his fourth string to B. This is obtained by matching the pitch of the eighth fret of the fourth string with that of the open third string.

Tuning: g BGBD

Arranged by Hank Sapoznik

Track 37

The Tailor's Twist

Key: C Major
(Fiddler plays in D: capo-2)

An exquisite double-fiddle version of this Irish hornpipe can be heard on *Andy McGann and Paddy Reynolds* (Shanachie 29004). The arrangement below, which includes most of the ornamentation that an Irish fiddler would use, is for accomplished clawhammerers only.

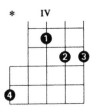

Tuning: g CGCD

Track 38

Reels

Reels are cut-time tunes based on a structure of eight even eighth notes per measure, organized in two groups of four. The first note of the first group receives the strongest accent, while the first note of the second group gets a somewhat weaker accent.

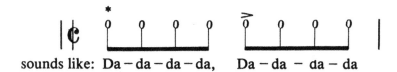

sounds like: Da – da – da – da,   Da – da – da – da

The last measure of each section ordinarily ends with two eighth-note pairs and a quarter note.

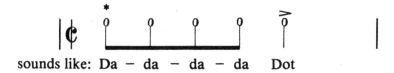

sounds like: Da – da – da – da   Dot

Reels must be played at a fast tempo and with considerable drive in order to give set dancers sufficient lift and energy for performing their figures. In fact, most reel melodies tend to sound flat and uninteresting when played slowly. On the banjo, the feeling of drive is obtained by bearing down heavily on accented notes while letting up considerably for notes between accents. In addition, the pivoting action on the upbeat preceding each primary accent must be particularly strong.

The manner in which reels are played varies greatly from region to region. English and New England fiddlers play their virtually unornamented reels with an almost bouncy feel to them. Irish fiddlers, on the other hand, play reels with extreme drive and ornament them heavily with grace notes, double grace notes, and Irish rolls. In recent years a style has developed in County Sligo, Ireland, which requires the musician to invent variations on a basic reel melody for each repetition.

Reels (and New-England-style hornpipes) consist of one phrase per measure, centering around the first accented note. The phrase begins at the preceding pivot note, and continues to a point just before the next pivot note. So, although reels are written:

Tuning: g DGBD

sounds like: Da–da–da–da, Da–da–da–da,   Da–da–da–da, Da–da–da–da,   Da–

They are played:

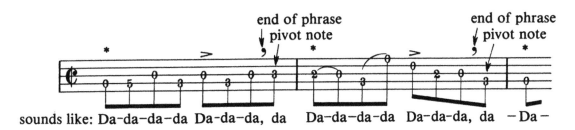

sounds like: Da–da–da–da Da–da–da, da   Da–da–da–da Da–da–da, da   – Da –

The Temperance Reel

Also called "The Teatotaller," this nineteenth century tune is very popular in present day New England and Ireland. It is related to a Kerry polka called "Pigtown" which is known at "The Pigtown Fling" in New England, and as "Stony Point" in the Galax area of Virginia. "The Temperance Reel" is printed in *O'Neill's Music of Ireland* and in Cole's *One Thousand Fiddle Tunes.* It can be heard on *The Hammered Dulcimer: Bill Spence and the Fennigs All Star Band* (Front Hall Records 01).

Tuning: g DGBD

Track 39

Jeff Davis

Jeff initially patterned his style on the playing of Frank Proffitt, an Appalachian master of the fretless banjo (see Folkways FA2360, *Frank Proffitt Sings Folk Songs).* Later influences included clawhammerer Tommy Thompson (of the Red Clay Ramblers) and fiddler Alan Jabbour. Jeff's current playing is characterized by a soft, sweet touch. He is only a part-time melodic player, being more concerned with capturing the feeling of a tune than with playing all its notes. Nowadays, Jeff teaches banjo at the Guitar Workshop (Roslyn, NY) and plays in a string band called Skunk's Misery. He can be heard (with friend Jeff Warner) on *Days of '49* (Minstrel JD 206).

Farrell O'Gara's Favorite

Jeff learned this tune from Cole's *One Thousand Fiddle Tunes.* He tells me that the same melody is printed elsewhere in *Cole's* under the titles "Old Joe Sife" and "Last Night's Fun." It also appears in *O'Neill's Music of Ireland* where it is called "The Macroom Lasses." By comparing Jeff's arrangement of "Farrell O'Gara's" with a printed version, it can be seen how he plays around the melody, yet still manages to come up with a coherent banjo piece.

Tuning: g DGBD

Arranged by Jeff Davis

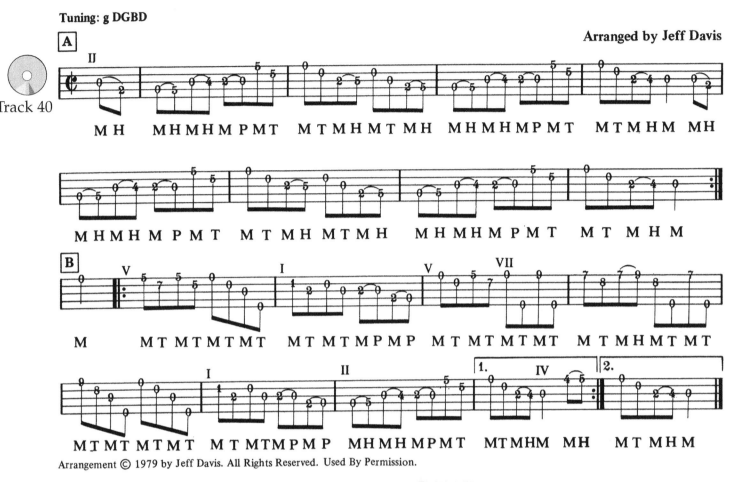

The Musical Priest

Key: G Dorian
(Fiddler plays in B: capo-4)

This is one of the very few Irish tunes played by the fiddler in the key of B Dorian. Printed in both the *Armagh Piper's Club Tune Book* and *O'Neill's Music of Ireland,* "The Musical Priest" can be heard on *Andy McGann and Paddy Reynolds* (Shanachie 29004). Note that it is made up of three four-measure sections, instead of the usual pattern for reels (two eight-measure sections).

Tuning: g DGCD

Track 41

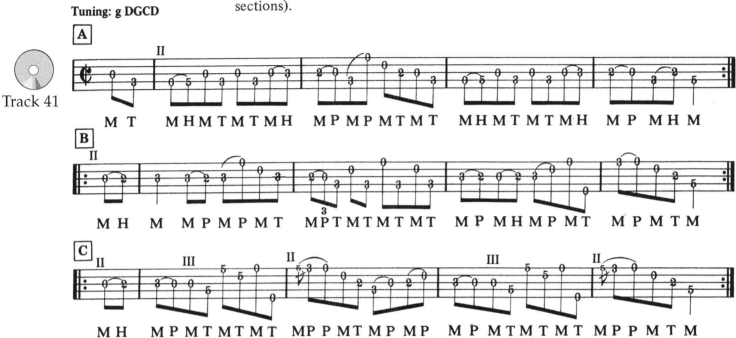

Allan Block and Ralph Lee Smith

The Mason's Apron

Key: G Major
(Fiddler plays in A: capo-2)

Sean Maguire, a well known Irish fiddler, has composed numerous variations on the basic theme of this Scottish tune. Maguire was heavily influenced by American music, so many of these variations are patterned on such styles as bluegrass, ragtime, and western swing. "The Mason's Apron" is printed in both Cole's *One Thousand Fiddle Tunes* and *O'Neill's Music of Ireland.* It can be heard, with some Maguire-like variations, on *The Boys of the Lough—Second Album* (Rounder 3006).

Tuning: g DGBD

Track 42

Ships Are Sailing

Key: D Dorian
(Fiddler plays in E: capo-2)

This reel is very popular among Irish musicians in New York City. It is printed in *O'Neill's Music of Ireland* and can be heard on *Johnny Cronin and Joe Burke* (Shanachie 29005). The Red Clay Ramblers do a version of "Ships" on *Merchant's Lunch* (Flying Fish FF055).

Tuning: g CGCD

Track 43

Rakish Paddy

Key: C Mixolydian
(Fiddler plays in D: capo-2)

This tune, which I learned from Irish fiddler Jim McIntyre, is related to a Scottish reel called "Caber Feidh" ("The Staghorns"). Like many Irish tunes played by the fiddler in D Mixolydian (D E F♯G A B C D), "Rakish Paddy" contains several C♯'s in its basic melody. As the presence of C♯ would ordinarily imply a D Major scale, this note is never permitted to fall on an accented beat. A version of this tune by fiddler James Morrisson can be heard on *The Wheels of the World* (Morning Star 45001).

Tuning: g CGCD

Track 44

Playing in ⁶⁄₈ Time—Jigs

Jigs are written in ⁶⁄₈ time which means that each measure can contain as many as six eighth notes. These eighth notes are organized in two groups of three, with an accent falling on the first note of each group.

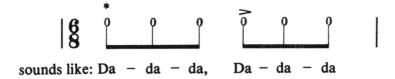

sounds like: Da − da − da,   Da − da − da

A quarter note can be substituted for any two eighth notes, yielding the following:

sounds like: Dot   −   da   Dot   −   da

A dotted quarter note can replace either an eighth-note grouping or a quarter-eighth combination.

In ⁶⁄₈ time, tunes made up primarily of quarter-eighth combinations are called *single jigs,* while those made up mostly of eighth-note groupings are called *double jigs.*

Jigs are usually played at a moderate to fast tempo. English and New England fiddlers tend to give them a lilting, lyrical feel. Irish fiddlers, on the other hand, play their jigs with heavy ornamentation, and with almost as much drive as reels. Until recently it was generally believed that jigs could not be played in clawhammer style. Actually, the playing of jigs presents no particular problem to the melodic player, although some ingenuity is required in arranging them properly. The trick to arranging jigs or any other type of tune for claw-hammering is in listening very closely to a fiddler's bowing patterns. It is then relatively simple to set your notes on the banjo in such a way that a similar feel is obtained.

Jigs have one phrase per measure built around the first and strongest note (downbeat). The phrase begins at the preceding pivot note and continues to a point just before the next pivot note. So, although jigs are written:

Tuning: g DGBD

sounds like: Da − da − da,   Da − da − da,   Da − da − da, Da − da − da,   Da −

The actual sound is:

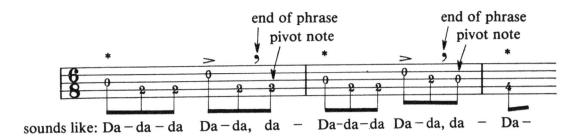

sounds like: Da – da – da   Da – da,   da   –   Da-da–da   Da – da, da   –   Da –

Performing H's and P's after Quick Slides

In the first measure of "Behind the Bush in the Garden" we have the following figure:

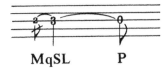

MqSL   P

In order to have sufficient sound to make a pull-off (or hammer-on) audible in situations like this, full pressure must be maintained on the target fret of the qSL, until the P (or H) is begun.

Behind the Bush in the Garden

Key: G Aeolian
(Fiddler plays in A: capo-2)

This Irish single jig has the same melody as a Scottish song called "We Have No King but Charley." It is also melodically related to the string band tune "Kitchen Girl" (p. 38) and to a Northumbrian double jig called "Elsie Marley" (see *Fingerpicking Fiddle Tunes)*. "Behind the Bush in the Garden" can be heard on *Andy McGann and Paddy Reynolds* (Shanachie 29004).

Tuning: g DGCD

Track 45

The Swallowtail Jig

Key: E Dorian

Known in Ireland as "The Swallow's Nest," this mid-nineteenth century double jig is often used to accompany Northumbrian sword dancing. (This involves a set of five men who perform complicated figures while holding on to five crossed two-handled swords.) "Swallowtail" is printed in Cole's *One Thousand Fiddle Tunes* and in *Allen's Irish Fiddler.*

Tuning: g DGBD

Track 46

The Blarney Pilgrim

Key: G Major

The town of Blarney, located in Ireland's County Kerry, is the home of the famed Blarney Stone which has attracted visitors from all over Ireland for centuries. It is said that anyone who kisses the Blarney Stone will be blessed with the gift of eloquence. However, since the stone is actually part of the wall of a medieval castle, it can only be reached by those courageous enough to dangle head first out of the nearest castle window. "The Blarney Pilgrim" is printed in *O'Neill's Music of Ireland* and can be heard on *Paul Brady and Andy Irvine* (Mulligan LUN00H).

Tuning: g DGBD

Track 47

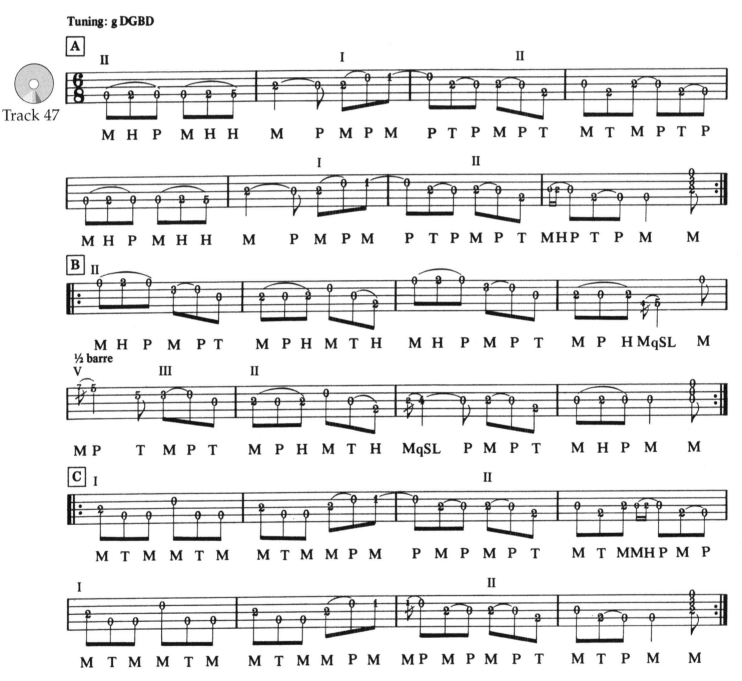

Banish Misfortune

Key: C Mixolydian
(Fiddler plays in D: capo-2)

"Banish Misfortune" is one of the best fiddle-tune melodies of all time. Like "Rakish Paddy" (p. 77) this Irish D Mixolydian tune contains several C♯'s on unaccented beats. It has extremely eccentric phrasing, so it took a lot of work to capture the feeling of this tune for clawhammer. The Chieftains do a fine version of "Banish Misfortune" on their #2 album (Claddagh TA4).

Tuning: g CGCD

Track 48

Novelty Tunes

(Just About) Everything You Ever Wanted to Play in Clawhammer Style, But Were Afraid to Try

Broken Chords

This technique (𝄇) is essentially a half roll (see p. 37). It involves a slow, controlled brush that covers three or four strings in the space of one beat.

Erick Frandsen

Erik Frandsen, who is one of the best finger-style guitar players around, also plays an interesting clawhammer banjo style. When Erik composed "Chamberlain Road" he was more influenced by Delta blues and by his own style of guitar picking than he was by traditional fiddle music. The result is the mournful, rhythmically complex piece below.

Chamberlain Road

Key: G Dorian

Tuning: g DGCD

By Erik Frandsen

Track 49

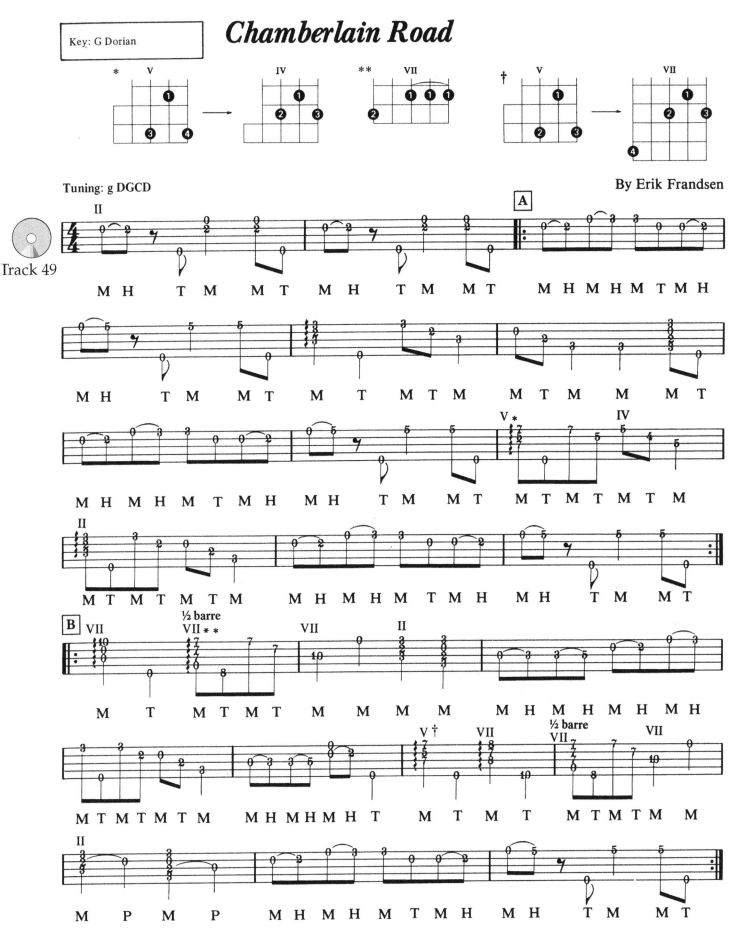

The Thumb-Over Technique

Until I saw Eric Mintz do it I was convinced that it was impossible to perform an M-T combination in which the T-note was on a higher long string than the M-note. In other words, Eric has found a way of obtaining the following types of figures:

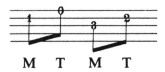

M   T   M   T

I don't do *thumb-overs* (T/O) myself, but Eric and I put our heads together and came up with the following series of exercises designed to gradually prepare your hand for the T/O technique.

First try the following:

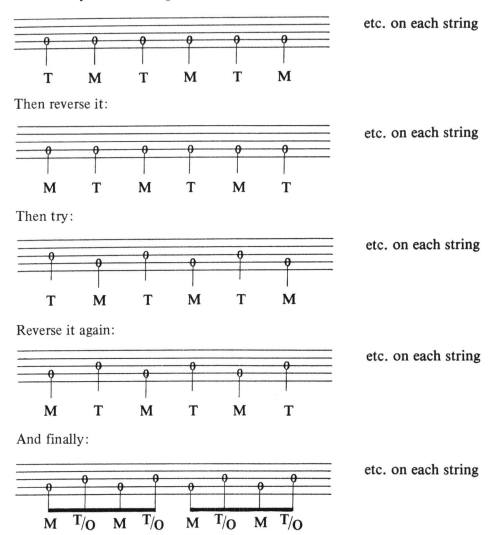

etc. on each string

T   M   T   M   T   M

Then reverse it:

etc. on each string

M   T   M   T   M   T

Then try:

etc. on each string

T   M   T   M   T   M

Reverse it again:

etc. on each string

M   T   M   T   M   T

And finally:

etc. on each string

M T/O M T/O M T/O M T/O

I intend to practice until I can perform my T/O's fluently, and recommend that you do the same. Meanwhile, for Eric's next piece, I've suggested (by means of broken lines and parentheses) alternative methods for obtaining his T/O notes.

Kemp's Jig

Key: C Major
(Always written in D:capo-2)

This tune dates from sixteenth century England, when the word *jig* referred to a type of dance, and not to a fiddle tune in $\frac{6}{8}$ time. Will Kemp, a member of Shakespeare's acting company, wagered that he could dance a jig all the way from London to Norwich, a distance of about one hundred miles. Kemp made the distance in nine days, resting each night at a local inn, and won the bet. "Kemp's Jig," which commemorates this event, is a favorite among present day classical guitarists.

Tuning: g CGBD

Arranged by Eric Mintz

Track 50

Arrangement © 1979 by Eric Mintz. All Rights Reserved. Used By Permission.

Playing in ¾ Time

In ¾ time, each measure has three beats, and each quarter note is counted as one beat. So, as many as three quarter notes can occur per measure. The accent is always on the first beat:

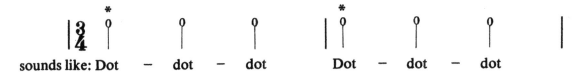

sounds like: Dot – dot – dot   Dot – dot – dot

A half note can be substituted for any two quarter notes, and a dotted half note can take the place of any three quarter notes.

Any quarter note can be replaced by two eighth notes, or an eighth note triplet.

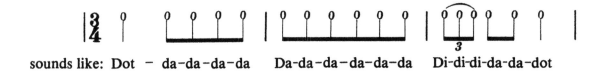

sounds like: Dot – da-da-da-da   Da-da-da-da-da-da   Di-di-di-da-da-dot

Planxty Lord Inchiquin

Key: C Major
(Harper plays in D: capo-2)

Carolan was a famous Irish harper of the early eighteenth century. He earned a good part of his living by composing *planxty* tunes for the noblemen who provided him with room, board, and pocket money. ("Planxty" is a Gaelic word meaning roughly "in honor of" or "dedicated to.") Printed in *O'Neill's Music of Ireland*, "Lord Inchiquin" can be heard on *The Chieftains #3* (Claddagh TA5).

By Carolan

Tuning: g CGCD

Track 51

O'Carolan's Concerto

Key: C Major
(Harper plays in D: capo-2)

It is said that a famous Italian violinist visited Ireland in Carolan's time, met the master harper and played Vivaldi's Fifth Concerto for him. Carolan immediately declared that he could compose his own concerto, and came up with the lovely tune printed below. "Carolan's Concerto" appears in *O'Neill's Music of Ireland* and can be heard on *The Chieftains #3* (Claddagh TA5).

By Carolan

Tuning: g CGCD

Track 52

Tied Notes

When a *tie* (a curved line) connects two or more notes of the same pitch, these are allowed to ring from the beginning of the first note to the end of the last tied note. The first note should not be re-struck.

The Mineola Rag

Keys: Parts A&B: C Major
Part C: F Major
(Fiddler plays in D and
G: capo-2)

Rags were originally designed for the piano, but by the 1920s many string bands were composing and recording ragtime pieces of their own. "Mineola Rag," named for Mineola, Texas, was one such fiddle rag. It was written and first recorded by a string band called the East Texas Serenaders. It is often difficult to obtain the highly syncopated rhythms of ragtime in clawhammer style, so I had to use nearly every trick I knew to make the phrasing of this arrangement come out right. Be sure to review the section on syncopation before proceeding.

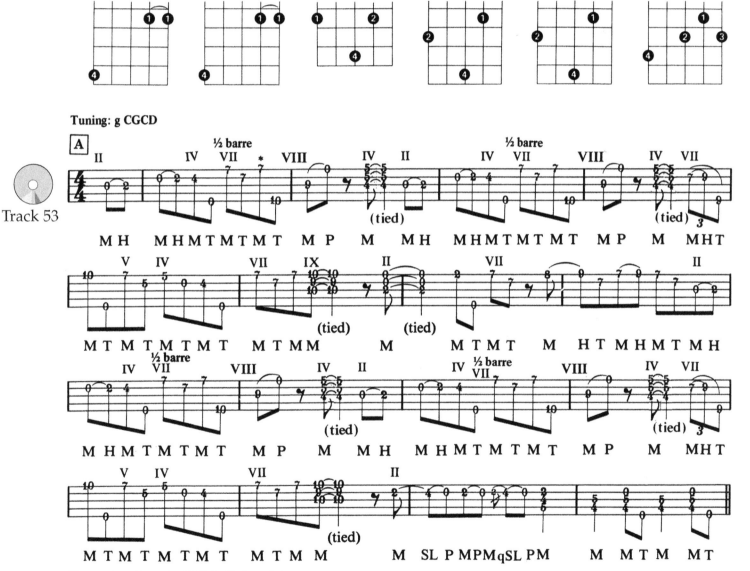

Tuning: g CGCD

Track 53

Tenor Chorale Theme
from Cantata #140 by J. S. Bach

Keys: Starts in C Major
but ends in G Major.
(Original score runs
from E♭ to A♭ : capo-3)

I recently attended a course in music history at a local college. The course was boring and poorly taught, but the professor earned my eternal gratitude by introducing me to this Bach theme, which was composed as one of a number of backgrounds to a Lutheran chorale known as "Wachet Auf." I have simplified the notation by writing the piece in cut time instead of the original $\frac{4}{4}$. This allowed me to do away with sixteenth notes, eighth rests, and hard-to-read syncopations. To maintain the same feel as the original, I have indicated that odd-number measures are to get primary accents (*), while even-number measures are to receive secondary accents (➤). *Cantata #140* is printed in *The Norton Scores: An Anthology for Listening,* and can be heard on *Johann Sebastian Bach: Cantatas #140 and #4* (Vanguard HM 20SD).

Tuning: g CGCD

Track 54

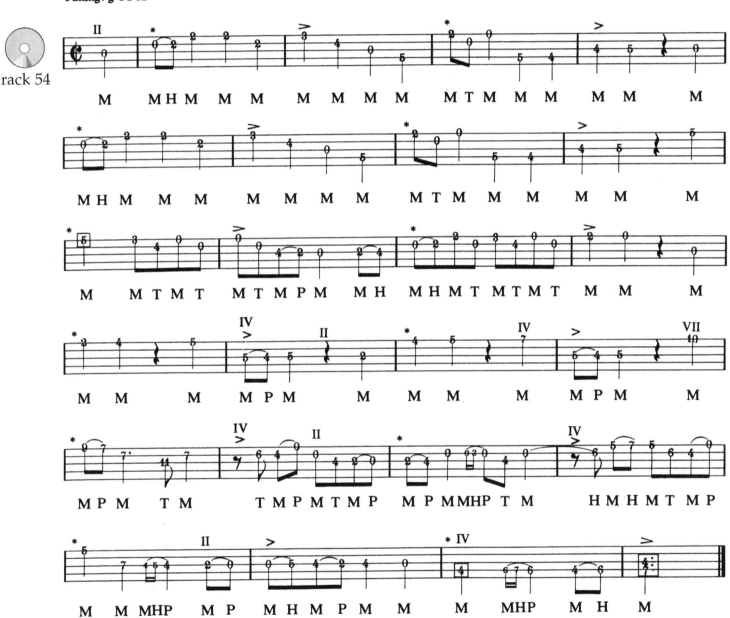

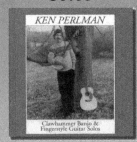

Those using
Centerstream
Books, Videos
& DVDs

The Competition

Centerstream Publishing
P.O Box 17878- Anaheim Hills, CA 92817

5-STRING BANJO CHORD CHART
by Ron Middlebrook
The only chart showing the open and moveable chord positions. Explains the two main playing styles, bluegrass and clawhammer, and includes a fingerboard chart.
00000074 .... $2.50

5 STRING BANJO NATURAL STYLE
No Preservatives
by Ron Middlebrook
Now available with a helpful play-along CD, this great songbook for 5-string banjo pickers features 10 easy, 10 intermediate and 10 difficult arrangements of the most popular bluegrass banjo songs. This book/CD pack comes complete with a chord chart.
00000284 Book/CD Pack $17.95

CLASSICAL BANJO
INCLUDES TAB
40 Classical Works Arranged for the 5-String Banjo
by Kyle R. Datesman
40 works from the Renaissance and Elizabethan period presented in chordal and a more linear manner. Includes an informative introduction about the origins of the music and playing style.
00000179 .... $12.95

BEGINNING CLAWHAMMER BANJO
DVD
by Ken Perlman
Ken Perlman is one of the most celebrated clawhammer banjo stylists performing today. In this new DVD, he teaches how to play this exciting style, with ample close-ups and clear explanations of techniques such as: hand positions, chords, tunings, brush-thumb, single-string strokes, hammer-ons, pull-offs and slides. Songs include: Boatsman • Cripple Creek • Pretty Polly. Includes a transcription booklet. 60 minutes.
00000330 DVD $19.95

INTERMEDIATE CLAWHAMMER BANJO
DVD
by Ken Perlman
Picking up where *Beginning Clawhammer Banjo* leaves off, this DVD begins with a review of brush thumbing and the single-string stroke, then moves into specialized techniques such as: drop- and double-thumbing, single-string brush thumb, chords in double "C" tuning, and more. Tunes include: Country Waltz • Green Willis • Little Billie Wilson • Magpie • The Meeting of the Waters • Old Joe Clark • and more! Includes a transcription booklet. 60 minutes.
00000331 DVD $19.95

CLAWHAMMER STYLE BANJO
DVD INCLUDES TAB
A Complete Guide for Beginning and Advanced Banjo Players
by Ken Perlman
The handbook on how to play the banjo. Covers basic right & left-hand positions, simple chords, and fundamental clawhammer techniques: the brush, the "bumm-titty" strum, pull-offs, and slides. For advanced players, there is instruction on more complicated picking, double thumbing, quick slides, fretted pull-offs, harmonics, improvisation, and more. The book includes over 40 fun-to-play banjo tunes.
00000118 Book Only $19.95
00000334 DVD $39.95

THE CLASSIC DOUGLAS DILLARD SONGBOOK OF 5-STRING BANJO TABLATURES
INCLUDES TAB
Published by popular demand, this long-awaited songbook contains exact transcriptions in banjo tablature that capture the unique playing style of Douglas Dillard. This fantastic collection includes all of his best-loved tunes, from the Andy Griffith Show, from his many great years of recording as the original Dillards, and from his solo banjo albums and his releases with The Doug Dillard Band. Features more than 20 tunes in G tuning, C tuning amd G modal tuning, including classics such as: Cripple Creek • Hickory Hollow • Jamboree • John Henry • Old Joe Clark • Buckin' Mule • and more. A must-have for all banjo players!
00000286 .... $19.95

THE EARLY MINSTREL BANJO
INCLUDES TAB
by Joe Weidlich
Featuring more than 65 classic songs, this interesting book teaches how to play the minstrel banjo like players who were part of various popular troupes in 1865. The book includes: a short history of the banjo in the US in the antebellum period, including the origins of the minstrel show; info on the construction of minstrel banjos, evolution of the lower-pitched minstrel banjo tunings, and idiomatic techniques peculiar to the minstrel banjo; chapters on each of the seven major banjo methods published through the end of the Civil War; songs from each method in banjo tablature, many available first time; info on how to arrange songs for the minstrel banjo; a reference list of contemporary gut and nylon string gauges approximating historical banjo string tensions in common usage during the antebellum period (for those Civil War re-enactors who wish to achieve that old-time "minstrel banjo" sound); and an extensive cross-reference list of minstrel banjo song titles found in the major antebellum banjo methods. (266 pages)
00000325 .... $29.95

THE BANJO MUSIC OF TONY ELLIS
INCLUDES TAB
One of Bill Monroe's Bluegrass Boys in the 1960s, Tony Ellis is among the most renowned banjo players around. This superb book assembles songs from four highly acclaimed CDs – Dixie Banner, Farewell My Home, Quaker Girl and Sounds like Bluegrass to Me – capturing his unique two- and three-finger playing techniques in the bluegrass style in standard notation and tab.
00000326 .... $19.95

GOSPEL BANJO
INCLUDES TAB
arranged by Dennis Caplinger
Features 15 spiritual favorites, each arranged in 2 different keys for banjo. Includes: Amazing Grace • Crying Holy • I'll Fly Away • In the Sweet By and By • Just a Closer Walk with Thee • Life's Railway to Heaven • Nearer My God to Thee • Old Time Religion • Swing Low, Sweet Chariot • Wayfaring Stranger • Will the Circle Be Unbroken • more!
00000249 .... $9.95

MINSTREL BANJO – BRIGGS' BANJO INSTRUCTOR
INCLUDES TAB
by Joseph Weidlich
The Banjo Instructor by Tom Briggs, published in 1855, was the first complete method for banjo. It contained "many choice plantation melodies," "a rare collection of quaint old dances," and the "elementary principles of music." This edition is a reprinting of the original Briggs' *Banjo Instructor*, made up-to-date with modern explanations, tablature, and performance notes. It teaches how to hold the banjo, movements, chords, slurs and more, and includes 68 banjo solo songs that Briggs presumably learned directly from slaves.
00000221 .... $12.95

MORE MINSTREL BANJO
INCLUDES TAB
by Joseph Weidlich
This is the second book in a 3-part series of intabulations of music for the minstrel (Civil War-era) banjo. Adapted from Frank Converse's *Banjo Instructor, Without a Master* (published in New York in 1865), this book contains a choice collection of banjo solos, jigs, songs, reels, walk arounds, and more, progressively arranged and plainly explained, enabling players to become proficient banjoists. Thorough measure-by-measure explanations are provided for each of the songs, all of which are part of the traditional minstrel repertoire.
00000258 .... $12.95

Book's and DVD's from Centerstream Publishing
P.O Box 17878- Anaheim Hills, CA 92817
centerstrm@aol.com